Don't Go Broke Paying for College

Smart Ways for Students and Parents to Save, Earn, and Graduate without Student Loans

Patty R. Adams

Table of Contents

Thank You for Reading!

I hope you found *Don't Go Broke Paying for College* helpful and enjoyable!

Your feedback is invaluable to me and helps others discover this book.

If you could take a moment to **leave a review**, I'd greatly appreciate it. Scan the QR code below to leave your review:

Thank you,

Patty R. Adams

Introduction

As both a parent who navigated the complex world of college financing and a high school counselor who has guided hundreds of families through this journey, I know firsthand that planning for college can feel overwhelming. The rising costs of higher education, combined with the maze of financial aid options, scholarship opportunities, and loan decisions, can leave even the most organized families feeling lost and anxious about their children's future.

This book serves as your comprehensive guide through the college financing journey, designed specifically for parents of students in grades 8-12 and the students themselves. Whether you're just beginning to explore college options or already deep into the planning process, you'll find practical strategies and actionable steps to make higher education more affordable.

Think of this guide as your family's financial planning companion throughout the high school years. Each chapter builds upon the last, helping you develop a personalized approach to college funding that aligns with your family's unique circumstances and goals. From maximizing need-based aid through strategic FAFSA planning to discovering hidden scholarship opportunities, from leveraging dual credit programs to understanding the true costs and benefits of different educational paths, we'll explore every avenue to reduce college costs while maintaining educational quality.

I've witnessed too many families make costly mistakes simply because they didn't have access to the right information at the right time. Like the Martinez family, who came to my office convinced they had started too late to make a difference in their twins' college funding. Through careful planning and strategic decisions, they not only found ways to reduce costs but also discovered opportunities they never knew existed. Their success story, along with many others you'll read about, demonstrates that it's never too late to implement effective college funding strategies.

What sets this guide apart is its focus on practical, real-world solutions combined with insider knowledge from both sides of the college planning equation. You'll learn not just what to do, but why and when to do it. We'll explore everything from 529 plans to military benefits, from athletic scholarships to work-study programs, and from dual credit opportunities to smart student loan decisions.

The path to affordable higher education isn't about having more money; it's about making smarter choices with the resources you have. Throughout this book, you'll find clear explanations, step-by-step guidance, and proven strategies that have helped hundreds of families achieve their college dreams without crushing debt. Consider this your roadmap to navigating the complex landscape of college financing, helping you transform what often feels like an insurmountable challenge into an achievable goal.

Let's begin this journey together, exploring how strategic planning, informed decisions, and creative approaches can open the door to affordable higher education for your family. Whether your student is a high academic achiever, a dedicated athlete, or a C-student with professional aspirations, this guide will help you discover and leverage opportunities that align with their unique strengths and circumstances.

Remember, every family's journey to college affordability is unique, but the principles and strategies we'll explore together have proven successful across a wide range of situations. By the time you finish this book, you'll have a clear understanding of your options and a personalized plan to make college more affordable for your family. Let's take that first step toward turning the dream of a college education into a financial reality.

Chapter 1:

Starting Smart: Early College Planning from Birth to High School

The journey to college affordability begins long before the first college application is submitted or the first scholarship essay is written. As both a parent and high school counselor, I've witnessed how families who start planning early, even from birth, create significantly more opportunities and face less financial stress when their children reach college age. The reality is that successful college planning isn't just about having the most money saved; it's about making informed decisions at every stage of your child's academic journey. As I've learned through years of counseling families, some of the most impactful choices come long before college applications begin.

I often share the story of the Martinez family to illustrate this point. When I first met them at Jefferson High School, they were parents of ninth-grade twins who felt overwhelmed by the prospect of college expenses. Mrs. Martinez tearfully confided that they had only managed to save $1,000 for each child, believing they had already failed their children's future. However, their story demonstrates that it's never too late to implement effective strategies for college affordability.

Together, we developed a comprehensive three-year plan that combined academic opportunities with modest but consistent financial planning. We identified dual credit courses that would allow the twins to earn college credits while still in high school, researched summer enrichment programs with scholarship potential, and established monthly automatic deposits of $50 per child into 529 plans. This multi-faceted approach proved transformative.

By graduation, each twin had completed 24 college credits through dual enrollment, representing nearly $15,000 in future college cost savings. Their modest but regular 529 plan contributions, combined with family gift contributions, grew to $4,500 each. The Martinez family's journey from anxiety to empowerment reveals how combining strategic academic planning with even modest financial commitment can significantly impact college affordability.

In this chapter, we'll explore the fundamental building blocks of college financial planning, from birth through high school. We'll examine how early decisions shape future opportunities and discuss practical strategies that any family can implement, regardless of their starting point. Whether you're reading this with a newborn at home or a high school student beside you, you'll discover actionable steps to make college more affordable.

We'll delve into the power of compound interest through vehicles like 529 plans, explore the academic planning milestones that can reduce future college costs, and understand how to build a strong foundation for college success through each grade level. Most importantly, you'll learn that every step forward, no matter how small, builds toward your goal of making college affordable for your family.

Early Savings Vehicles: Understanding 529 Plans, Coverdell ESAs, and Investment Strategies

When it comes to saving for college, starting early with the right savings vehicle can make a profound difference in your family's financial future. Two of the most powerful tools available for college savings are 529 plans and Coverdell Education Savings Accounts (ESAs), each offering unique advantages that can help make higher education more affordable.

Let's begin with 529 plans, which have become increasingly popular due to their flexibility and generous contribution limits. These state-sponsored investment accounts allow your money to grow tax-free when used for qualified education expenses. Unlike many other savings vehicles, 529 plans have no annual contribution limits, though they do have lifetime limits that often reach several hundred thousand dollars per beneficiary. For example, if grandparents, parents, and other family members want to contribute, they can each give up to $13,000 annually ($26,000 for married couples) without triggering gift tax implications.

Qualified expenses for 529 plans cover a broad range of college costs, including tuition, fees, books, supplies, room and board, and even computer equipment and internet access. One of the most attractive features of 529 plans is that there are no income restrictions, making them accessible to families across all income levels. Additionally, many states offer tax deductions or credits for contributions to their state-sponsored 529 plans, providing immediate tax benefits alongside long-term growth potential.

Coverdell Education Savings Accounts offer a different set of advantages, particularly for families who want more control over their investment choices or need to cover K-12 education expenses. However, these accounts come with stricter limitations. The annual contribution limit is capped at $2,000 per beneficiary, and there are income restrictions that may prevent higher-earning families from participating. Contributions must stop when the beneficiary reaches 18, and the funds typically need to be used by age 30.

The power of starting early with either of these vehicles cannot be overstated. Consider this example: A family that invests $200 monthly in a 529 plan from their child's birth, assuming a 6% average annual return, would accumulate approximately $65,000 by the time their child turns 18. In contrast, waiting until the child is 10 years old and investing the same monthly amount would result in only about $23,000 by age 18.

For many families, a strategic approach might involve utilizing both savings vehicles. For instance, if you qualify for a Coverdell ESA, you might maximize its $2,000 annual contribution limit to take advantage of its broader qualified expense definition and investment flexibility, then direct additional savings to a 529 plan. This hybrid approach can provide the best of both worlds: the investment control and K-12 expense coverage of a Coverdell ESA, combined with the higher contribution limits and state tax benefits of a 529 plan.

When selecting a 529 plan, don't feel confined to your state's offering. While in-state plans may provide state tax benefits, you're free to choose any state's plan. Compare plans based on investment options, fees, and performance history. Look for plans that offer age-based portfolios, which automatically adjust to become more conservative as your child approaches college age, helping to protect your accumulated savings.

Regardless of which savings vehicle you choose, the key is to start as early as possible and contribute consistently. Even modest monthly contributions can grow significantly over time through the power of compound interest. Set up automatic monthly transfers to make saving a habit, and consider increasing your contributions whenever your income rises or you receive windfalls like tax refunds or bonuses.

Remember that these education savings vehicles are just one part of a comprehensive college funding strategy. They work best when combined with other approaches we'll discuss in later chapters, such as strategic academic planning, scholarship opportunities, and smart college selection. The goal is to build a strong financial foundation that gives your family options when it's time to make important decisions about higher education.

Academic Planning in K-12: Advanced Placement, Dual Credit, and Early College Programs

One of the most powerful strategies for reducing college costs begins well before setting foot on a college campus. Through careful academic planning during high school, students can earn significant college credits through dual credit programs and early college initiatives. These opportunities not only save thousands in future tuition costs but also help students develop college-ready skills and demonstrate academic rigor to admissions offices.

Dual credit programs, sometimes called dual enrollment, provide a valuable pathway to earning college credits during high school. These courses count simultaneously toward high school and college requirements through partnerships between high schools and local colleges. The cost savings can be dramatic; while a three-credit college course might cost $1,000 or more at a university, the same credits through dual enrollment often cost $100-300, with some programs even offering credits tuition-free.

Early College High School programs represent perhaps the most comprehensive approach to early college credit. These innovative programs allow students to earn both their high school diploma and up to two years of college credit, or even an associate degree, by graduation. These programs are particularly valuable for first-generation college students and those from low-income families, as they're typically offered at no additional cost to participants.

The key to maximizing these opportunities lies in early planning and strategic course selection. Students should begin exploring these options as early as 8th grade, working with counselors to develop a four-year plan that balances academic rigor with their other commitments. Course choices should align with intended college majors or general education requirements to ensure credits will transfer effectively.

When evaluating which programs to pursue, consider factors beyond just the potential credit earnings. Dual credit courses provide direct experience with college-level coursework in a supported environment. Research shows that students who succeed in these advanced programs are more likely to graduate college on time, further reducing total education costs.

It's essential to maintain open communication with both high school counselors and prospective colleges throughout this process. Counselors can help evaluate a student's readiness for advanced coursework and ensure proper course sequencing. Meanwhile, college admissions offices can provide current information about credit transfer policies and program recognition.

The financial impact of these programs extends beyond direct tuition savings. By entering college with credits already completed, students may be able to graduate early, reducing not just tuition costs but also expenses for room, board, and other fees. Additionally, the academic preparation these programs provide can help students avoid costly remedial courses in college, which often don't count toward degree requirements but still incur tuition charges.

While these programs offer tremendous benefits, it's important to maintain balance. Students should carefully consider their academic strengths, extracurricular commitments, and personal well-being when deciding how many advanced courses to take. Success in these programs requires dedicated study time and strong organizational skills. The goal is to challenge yourself appropriately while maintaining academic success across all courses.

By thoughtfully incorporating dual credit options and early college programs into your high school planning, you can significantly reduce future college costs while building a strong foundation for higher education success. The key is to start planning early, research options thoroughly, and maintain regular communication with counselors and college admissions offices to ensure your choices align with your educational and financial goals.

Building a Strong Foundation: Grade-by-Grade Financial and Academic Milestones

Success in college planning isn't just about saving money; it's about making informed decisions at every stage of your child's academic journey. From birth through high school graduation, each year presents unique opportunities to build a strong foundation for affordable higher education. By understanding and acting on these grade-by-grade milestones, families can maximize their chances of achieving their college funding goals while minimizing potential debt.

The journey begins in early childhood, where establishing good financial habits can have profound long-term effects. Even modest monthly contributions to a 529 plan or custodial account during these years can grow significantly through compound interest. For example, investing just $100 monthly from birth in a 529 plan with a conservative 5% annual return could grow to over $35,000 by the time your child reaches college age. During these early years, it's also crucial to foster a love of learning through reading and basic math skills, which will form the foundation for future academic success.

As children enter middle school, the focus shifts to more concrete academic and financial planning. This is the time to begin discussions about different types of colleges and their associated costs. Middle school students should start exploring their interests through extracurricular activities and community service experiences that can later translate into scholarship opportunities. It's also the perfect time to ensure students are on track with prerequisite courses for high school honors courses.

The transition to high school marks a critical phase in college preparation. Freshmen and sophomores should focus on maintaining strong GPAs while enrolling in rigorous courses that match their abilities. This is also the time to begin systematic scholarship searches; many national and local scholarships accept applications from underclassmen. Financially, students should learn practical money management skills by opening their first checking or savings account and tracking their spending.

Junior and senior years require careful balancing of academic excellence with college planning activities. Students should take challenging courses while researching colleges that offer strong programs in their areas of interest. This is the time to visit campuses, attend college fairs, and create a strategic list of schools based on both academic fit and affordability. Understanding the FAFSA process becomes crucial during these years, as does applying for scholarships systematically.

Throughout all grade levels, regular communication between parents and students about college goals and financial realities is essential. These conversations should evolve from simple discussions about saving money in elementary school to more complex talks about college costs, career paths, and return on investment in high school. The key is maintaining open dialogue while working together toward shared educational goals.

For example, families should discuss the implications of different college choices well before application season begins. A student interested in engineering might compare the costs and outcomes of attending a prestigious private university versus a strong state school program. This analysis should include not just tuition differences but also potential scholarship opportunities, internship programs, and job placement rates.

Each academic year also presents opportunities for cost-saving strategies. High school students can reduce future college expenses by taking advantage of dual enrollment programs, where they earn college credits while still in high school. Some students might choose to take summer classes at a local community college to get ahead academically while saving money on future credits.

Financial milestones should be reviewed and adjusted annually. Families should reassess college savings plans, adjust contribution amounts if possible, and explore additional funding sources as they become available. This might include encouraging relatives to contribute to college funds for birthdays or holidays instead of traditional gifts, or researching employer tuition benefits that could help offset costs.

The goal of this grade-by-grade approach is to create a comprehensive strategy that combines academic excellence with financial preparedness. By following these milestones, families can work systematically toward making college affordable while ensuring students are prepared for academic success. Remember that it's never too early to start planning, and even small steps taken consistently can lead to significant results over time.

Each family's journey will be unique, but the fundamental principles remain the same: start early, stay consistent, and maintain open communication about both academic and financial goals. By treating college preparation as a gradual process rather than a last-minute scramble, families can maximize their opportunities while minimizing stress and potential debt. As we conclude this chapter on early college planning, it's clear that the path to affordable higher education begins long before the college application process. The stories and strategies we've explored demonstrate that success comes not from having the most money saved, but from making informed decisions consistently throughout your child's academic journey.

Whether you're starting your college planning journey with a newborn or a high school student, remember the key lessons we've covered. Early financial planning through vehicles like 529 plans and Coverdell ESAs can harness the power of compound interest to grow even modest contributions significantly over time. Strategic academic planning during the K-12 years can substantially reduce future college costs while preparing students for college-level work.

The Martinez family's story reminds us that it's never too late to implement effective strategies. By combining consistent financial planning with strategic academic choices, they transformed their children's college prospects despite a late start. Their success demonstrates how the principles we've discussed, from regular 529 plan contributions to maximizing dual credit opportunities, can work together to make college more affordable.

As you move forward with your own college planning journey, remember to:

- Start saving early, even if only small amounts initially
- Take advantage of compound interest through appropriate savings vehicles
- Research and utilize grade-appropriate academic opportunities
- Maintain open communication about college goals and financial realities
- Regularly assess and adjust your college savings strategy

Perhaps most importantly, recognize that successful college planning is a gradual process that combines financial preparation with academic readiness. Every step forward, whether opening a college savings account or exploring dual credit opportunities, builds toward your goal of making higher education affordable.

In the chapters ahead, we'll explore more specific strategies for maximizing financial aid, securing scholarships, and selecting colleges that offer the best value for your educational investment. The foundation you build through early planning will make these later steps more effective and your ultimate goal of affordable higher education more achievable.

Remember, the journey to affordable college education is a marathon, not a sprint. By implementing the strategies we've discussed and maintaining consistent focus on both academic and financial preparation, you're already on the path to making college more affordable for your family.

Chapter 2:

The Strategic Student: Maximizing High School for College Credit

The most overlooked opportunity to slash college costs lies not in financial aid forms or scholarship applications, but in the strategic choices students make during their high school years. Every credit hour earned before college matriculation represents both a financial victory and an academic advantage, potentially saving thousands in future tuition costs while building college-ready skills. These early choices can shape not just academic outcomes but also financial futures, making it crucial to understand all available options for earning college credits during high school years.

As both a counselor and advocate for affordable education, I've seen firsthand how strategic academic planning in high school can dramatically reduce the overall cost of a college degree. The opportunities available through Advanced Placement (AP) courses, dual enrollment programs, and early college initiatives represent more than just academic challenges; they're powerful tools for reducing future college costs.

During my years as a high school counselor, I worked with a determined student named Sarah who came from a family with limited financial resources. At our first meeting, she expressed anxiety about affording college, but was willing to put in the work to make it happen. Together, we crafted a strategic four-year plan that combined

AP classes with dual enrollment opportunities at our local community college. Sarah started with one AP class in her sophomore year to test the waters, then gradually increased her college-credit coursework. By carefully selecting courses that would transfer to her target universities, she managed to complete 36 college credits while still in high school. The total cost for these credits through our dual enrollment program was $2,400, compared to the potential $14,400 she would have paid at her chosen state university. Sarah's story exemplifies how strategic planning and dedication during high school can dramatically reduce college costs while building academic confidence. She not only saved money but also entered college with a full year of credits and a clear understanding of college-level expectations.

The key to maximizing these opportunities lies in understanding the unique advantages and considerations of each option. Advanced Placement courses offer standardized curricula recognized nationwide, while dual enrollment programs provide direct college credit experience. Early college programs can offer even more extensive opportunities for earning credits, though they require careful planning and strong academic dedication.

In this chapter, we'll explore how to evaluate which college credit opportunities best match your academic strengths and college goals. We'll examine the specific requirements, potential pitfalls, and strategies for success in each program type. Most importantly, we'll learn how to create a balanced plan that maximizes college credits while maintaining academic excellence and avoiding burnout.

By understanding these opportunities early in your high school career, you can make informed choices that significantly reduce your future college costs while building valuable academic skills. The strategies we'll discuss aren't just about saving money – they're about creating a stronger foundation for college success while developing the time management and study skills essential for higher education.

Advanced Placement (AP) vs. Dual Enrollment: Comparing Costs, Benefits, and Success Rates

When considering options for earning college credits in high school, two primary pathways emerge: Advanced Placement (AP) courses and dual enrollment programs. Each offers distinct advantages and considerations that can significantly impact both academic preparation and college costs. Understanding these differences is crucial for making strategic decisions that align with your educational goals and financial resources.

Advanced Placement courses follow a standardized curriculum developed by the College Board, culminating in an exam that costs between $97 and $145.[10] While this may seem like a significant expense, it's substantially less than traditional college course costs.[10] The standardized nature of AP programs means credits earned through high exam scores (typically 3 or higher on a 5-point scale) are widely recognized across institutions nationwide.[7] This standardization provides a reliable measure of college-level academic achievement that many universities trust.

Dual enrollment, by contrast, offers a different approach by allowing students to take actual college courses while still in high school. The costs vary significantly, ranging from completely free in some states to approximately $400 per course in others[10]. Unlike AP courses, which require passing a final exam for credit, dual enrollment credits are guaranteed upon successful course completion[7]. These credits appear directly on a college transcript, providing immediate progress toward a degree.[10]

Research has revealed interesting patterns in student success between these two pathways. Students who score 3 or higher on AP exams often demonstrate stronger academic performance in college, including higher first-year GPAs and better four-year persistence rates.[8] However, dual enrollment offers its own unique advantages, particularly in providing an authentic college classroom experience and guaranteed credits upon course completion.[10]

When choosing between these options, consider your learning style and academic strengths. AP courses might be more suitable if you excel at standardized testing and prefer the familiar high school environment. The structured curriculum and comprehensive exam preparation can provide excellent college readiness training. Dual enrollment, however, might be preferable if you want guaranteed credit upon course completion and value experiencing actual college classroom dynamics.[10]

A strategic approach often involves combining both options based on your specific circumstances. For example, you might take AP courses in subjects where you excel at standardized testing while pursuing dual enrollment in areas where you prefer regular classroom assessment. This hybrid approach allows you to maximize the benefits of both programs while minimizing their respective drawbacks.

When evaluating these opportunities, consider your target colleges' credit acceptance policies. While AP credits are widely recognized[7], dual enrollment credits may require more research to ensure transferability.[9] Some students find success by taking dual-enrollment courses through four-year institutions, as these credits often transfer more readily than those earned through two-year colleges.[8]

The financial implications of these choices can be substantial. Consider that each college credit earned in high school potentially saves hundreds or even thousands of dollars in future tuition costs.[10] For instance, a student who successfully completes several AP exams or dual enrollment courses might enter college with a semester or more of credits already completed, potentially reducing their time to graduation and overall educational expenses.

Regardless of which path you choose, early planning is essential. Begin researching these options as early as freshman year to ensure you can take full advantage of all available opportunities. Work closely with your school counselor to understand specific requirements, prerequisites, and timing considerations for both AP and dual-enrollment programs at your school.

Early College High School Programs: Maximizing Credits While Managing Course Load

Early College High School programs represent one of the most transformative opportunities for reducing college costs while accelerating academic achievement. These innovative programs allow students to earn up to 60 college credits, equivalent to two years of college coursework, while simultaneously completing their high school diploma.[14] For families concerned about college affordability, this pathway can significantly reduce the total cost of a bachelor's degree while providing students with valuable college experience.

The financial benefits of Early College programs are substantial and measurable. Students can earn college credits tuition-free or at minimal cost, potentially saving tens of thousands of dollars in future college expenses.[12, 14] Research demonstrates that the total benefits of these programs are 4.6 times their cost, making them an exceptionally sound investment in your educational future.[15] When you consider that each college credit earned through these programs represents hundreds of dollars in future tuition savings, the cumulative financial impact becomes clear.

However, success in Early College programs requires careful planning and strong support systems. Students must develop effective strategies for managing increased academic demands while maintaining balance in their educational journey. This often involves creating detailed study schedules, learning to prioritize assignments across both high school and college courses, and developing strong time management skills.[11] Many successful Early College students find that creating weekly planning sessions helps them stay on track with their dual academic responsibilities.

The program structure typically includes comprehensive academic counseling and support services designed specifically for dual-enrollment students.[14] These resources are crucial for helping students navigate the challenges of college-level coursework while still in high school. Students receive guidance on college systems, registration processes, and academic expectations, all while maintaining access to high school support structures.

One particularly valuable aspect of Early College programs is their focus on preparing students for long-term college success. Beyond just earning credits, participants develop essential college-ready skills and mindsets.[11] Research shows that Early College students experience higher high school graduation rates and are more likely to enroll in higher education after graduation. They also tend to have fewer disciplinary issues compared to peers in traditional high school programs.[13]

When considering an Early College program, it's essential to evaluate your readiness for college-level work and your ability to manage an increased academic load. Start by assessing your current academic performance, study habits, and time management skills.[11] Consider your extracurricular commitments and how they might need to be adjusted to accommodate a more demanding course schedule. Many successful Early College students find it helpful to gradually increase their college course load, starting with one or two classes before taking on a fuller schedule.

Communication with both high school and college instructors becomes particularly important in these programs. Successful students develop the habit of reaching out proactively when they need clarification or support, treating this as an opportunity to build professional communication skills that will serve them well in their future academic and professional careers.

The program's structure typically involves strong partnerships between high schools and higher education institutions, ensuring smooth credit transfer and recognition.[14] However, it's crucial to verify that the credits earned will transfer to your target universities. While most institutions accept these credits, policies can vary, making early research into credit transfer essential for maximizing the program's benefits.

For families concerned about college affordability, Early College High School programs offer a powerful strategy for reducing the overall cost of higher education while providing students with valuable college experience.[12, 14] The combination of tuition savings, academic preparation, and skill development makes these programs an attractive option for students ready to challenge themselves academically while working toward their college goals.

Strategic Course Selection: Building a Four-Year Plan for Maximum College Credit

Building a strategic four-year plan for maximum college credit requires careful planning, starting as early as freshman year. This comprehensive approach can significantly reduce college costs while providing students with valuable academic preparation. By understanding available options and planning course selections strategically, students can potentially earn up to 40 or more college credits before high school graduation, representing potential savings of $20,000-$30,000 in future college expenses.

The foundation of an effective four-year plan begins in freshman year, focusing on core academic requirements and honors-level courses that prepare students for more advanced work. During this crucial first year, students should research upcoming AP, IB, and dual credit options while meeting with guidance counselors to understand college credit policies. This early preparation sets the stage for increasingly challenging coursework in subsequent years.

Sophomore year marks the beginning of credit acceleration, with students typically starting their first AP courses in their strongest subject areas. This is also the time to explore dual enrollment eligibility requirements and identify target colleges' credit acceptance policies. Taking the PSAT during sophomore year provides valuable standardized test preparation while helping students gauge their readiness for college-level work.

Junior year represents a critical period for credit accumulation. Students should increase their AP or IB course load based on demonstrated academic strengths while beginning dual enrollment courses if available. Research shows that successful completion of these advanced courses not only saves money but also correlates with higher college graduation rates and academic success. During this year, students should also research CLEP exam opportunities for additional credit potential.

Senior year focuses on maximizing credit opportunities while aligning coursework with intended college majors. A strategic combination of AP courses and dual enrollment classes can help students enter college with significant credits already completed. Some students may even qualify for early graduation if they've accumulated sufficient credits, though this decision should be weighed carefully against other academic and extracurricular opportunities.

When implementing a four-year plan, families often face common challenges that require proactive solutions. Credit transfer concerns can be addressed by researching target colleges' acceptance policies early and focusing on core general education requirements that typically transfer more readily. Academic readiness issues are best managed by building gradually, starting with one or two advanced courses in stronger subjects before expanding the course load.

Scheduling conflicts, another common challenge, require working closely with counselors to prioritize the most valuable credit-earning opportunities. Some students find success by considering online or summer options when traditional scheduling proves difficult. For families concerned about AP exam costs, many schools offer fee reductions, and some states provide subsidies for low-income students.

To maximize the effectiveness of a four-year plan, regular communication with guidance counselors is essential to ensure credits align with college requirements. Students should maintain careful documentation of all earned credits and regularly research specific credit policies at their target colleges. This comprehensive approach to planning can significantly reduce both the time and money required to complete a college degree.[16]

The financial impact of strategic course selection is substantial and measurable. Consider that each AP course with a passing score (3 or higher) can translate to 3-4 college credits, potentially saving $1,500-$2,000 per course at many universities. Dual enrollment courses often offer even more direct savings, as they're frequently provided at reduced or no cost during high school. When combined effectively, these strategies can help students enter college with a semester or more of credits already completed, substantially reducing their total educational expenses.[5, 17]

Successful implementation of a four-year plan requires regular monitoring and adjustment. Students should review their progress each semester, adjusting their course selections based on academic performance and evolving college goals. This flexible approach ensures that students maintain a challenging but manageable course load while maximizing their college credit potential. As we conclude this chapter on maximizing high school opportunities for college credit, it's clear that the strategic choices students make during these formative years can dramatically impact their educational costs and outcomes. The combination of AP courses, dual enrollment programs, and Early College opportunities provides multiple pathways to reduce college expenses while building crucial academic skills.

Through Sarah's story, we witnessed how careful planning and dedication can lead to substantial savings - in her case, completing 36 college credits for $2,400 compared to the potential $14,400 cost at a state university. This example demonstrates the tangible financial benefits of taking advantage of these opportunities. However, the advantages extend beyond mere cost savings. Students who participate in these programs often develop stronger study skills, better time management abilities, and increased confidence in handling college-level work.

The key to success lies in creating a balanced, well-researched plan that aligns with your academic strengths and college goals. Whether choosing AP courses for their standardized recognition, dual enrollment for guaranteed credits, or participating in Early College programs for maximum credit potential, each path offers unique benefits that can significantly reduce the overall cost of a college degree.

As you move forward with your college preparation journey, remember that early planning is crucial. Start researching these opportunities as early as freshman year, maintain open communication with guidance counselors, and carefully consider how each credit-earning opportunity aligns with your intended college major and career goals. By taking a strategic approach to earning college credits in high school, you're not just saving money; you're investing in your academic future and building the skills necessary for college success.

Your chosen path may combine several of these options or focus primarily on one that best suits your circumstances. Whatever route you select, the time and effort invested in earning college credits during high school can yield significant returns, both financially and academically. As you implement these strategies, stay focused on maintaining academic excellence while managing your course load effectively. Remember, the goal isn't just to accumulate credits, but to build a strong foundation for your college education while reducing future costs.

In the next chapter, we'll explore how to navigate the FAFSA process effectively, adding another crucial tool to your college affordability toolkit. The strategies you've learned here for earning college credits will work hand-in-hand with financial aid opportunities to create a comprehensive approach to funding your education.

Chapter 3:

Navigating the FAFSA: Your Comprehensive Guide to Financial Aid

The FAFSA form stands between millions of students and billions of dollars in financial aid each year, yet many families leave money on the table by making simple mistakes or failing to apply at all. As a high school counselor who has guided hundreds of families through this process, I've learned that understanding the FAFSA isn't just about filling out a form; it's about positioning your family for maximum aid eligibility while avoiding common pitfalls that can cost thousands in lost opportunities. With billions in federal aid available each year, mastering the FAFSA process is crucial for unlocking access to grants, work-study opportunities, and federal loans. As I've learned through years of counseling experience, success with the FAFSA often comes down to understanding not just what information to provide, but how to present it in a way that accurately reflects your family's financial situation.

Last year, I worked with the Thompson family, who initially thought they wouldn't qualify for any financial aid because they owned a small business. During our first meeting, Mrs. Thompson showed me their rejected FAFSA from the previous year, which they had completed without guidance. Reviewing their application, I noticed they had incorrectly reported their business assets, significantly inflating their

Expected Family Contribution. We worked together to resubmit their FAFSA, properly documenting their business assets and liabilities according to federal guidelines. The result was transformative; their revised EFC qualified them for over $15,000 in need-based aid at their daughter's chosen state university. This experience taught them that understanding how to properly report assets and income on the FAFSA can dramatically impact aid eligibility. The Thompsons' story exemplifies why I'm passionate about helping families navigate this complex process, because sometimes, the difference between receiving substantial aid and none at all comes down to understanding how to accurately complete the form.

In this chapter, we'll break down the FAFSA process into manageable steps, helping you avoid common pitfalls that could cost your family thousands in potential aid. We'll explore how to gather the necessary documentation, understand key terminology, and time your application for maximum benefit. More importantly, we'll look at strategies for presenting your financial information in a way that gives you the best chance of receiving the aid you deserve.

Whether you're a family navigating the FAFSA for the first time or seeking to appeal a previous aid determination, this chapter will provide you with the tools and knowledge to approach the process with confidence. Remember, the FAFSA isn't just a form; it's your gateway to making college more affordable, and understanding how to complete it effectively can significantly impact your family's financial future.

FAFSA Fundamentals: Required Documents, Deadlines, and Step-by-Step Completion Guide

Successfully completing the FAFSA requires careful preparation and attention to detail. Before sitting down to complete the application, gather all necessary documentation to ensure accurate reporting of your financial information. This organized approach will streamline the process and help maximize your potential aid eligibility.

First, collect all personal identification documents. You'll need Social Security cards and driver's licenses for both the student and the parents (if the student is a dependent).[19] Non-U.S. citizens should have their Alien Registration card ready.[20] These documents ensure proper identification and eligibility verification for federal aid programs.

Next, assemble your financial records. For the 2025-26 academic year, you'll need your 2023 federal income tax returns. This includes W-2 forms and any other records of money earned.[20] Having your bank statements and records of investments readily available is crucial, as you'll need to report current balances and asset values. If you own a business or farm, gather documentation of their net worth.[18]

Timing is critical when submitting your FAFSA. While federal deadlines provide a final submission date, many colleges and states have much earlier priority filing dates that can affect aid availability.[21] Some financial aid is awarded on a first-come, first-served basis, making early submission vital for maximizing your aid opportunities. Check with each school's financial aid office for their specific priority deadlines, as missing these dates could mean missing out on institutional aid.

The IRS Data Retrieval Tool has revolutionized the FAFSA completion process by allowing automatic transfer of federal tax return information directly into your application. This tool not only reduces errors but also simplifies the verification process if your application is selected for review.[20] When available, always opt to use this tool as it provides the most accurate reporting of your tax information.

For dependent students, understanding what parent information to include is crucial. If your parents are divorced or separated, you'll need financial information from the parent you lived with most during the past 12 months.[21] If that parent has remarried, your stepparent's information must also be included. This requirement often surprises families, but is essential for accurate aid calculations.

Keep in mind that certain types of income and assets require special attention. Untaxed income, such as child support received,[19] welfare benefits, Social Security income, and veteran's benefits must be reported.[20] However, the value of your primary residence and retirement accounts should not be included as assets on the FAFSA.

If you haven't completed your taxes before the priority filing dates, you can estimate your income and other tax information. However, remember to correct your application after filing taxes to ensure accuracy.[20] Incorrect information can lead to adjustments in your aid package or, worse, the need to repay aid you've received.

The online FAFSA at fafsa.gov offers the fastest processing time and includes helpful tools and error checks. While a PDF version is available, electronic submission is highly recommended for its efficiency and accuracy.[21] The online form also provides immediate confirmation of submission, giving you peace of mind that your application is in process.

As financial aid expert Mark Kantrowitz notes, "The FAFSA is the gateway to virtually all financial aid—federal, state, and institutional. Even if you don't think you'll qualify for need-based aid, fill it out anyway. Many merit scholarships require the FAFSA, and some aid is first-come, first-served." This advice underscores the importance of completing the FAFSA regardless of your financial situation.

Remember that the FAFSA must be renewed each year you're in school. Set calendar reminders for gathering documents and submission deadlines to ensure you don't miss out on aid opportunities in subsequent years. Maintaining organized records of your submitted FAFSAs and supporting documents will make the renewal process much smoother.

Understanding and Optimizing Your Expected Family Contribution (EFC)

Understanding your Expected Family Contribution (EFC) is crucial for maximizing financial aid opportunities and developing a realistic college funding strategy. While the term may suggest it represents what your family must pay for college, the EFC actually serves as an index number that colleges use to determine your eligibility for federal, state, and institutional financial aid.[22, 24] This number can significantly impact the types and amounts of aid available to you, making it essential to understand how it's calculated and what steps you can take to optimize it.

The EFC calculation considers several key factors: your family's income, assets, size, and the number of family members attending college simultaneously. For the 2025-26 academic year, significant changes have been implemented in how this contribution is calculated,[23, 25,] but the fundamental principle remains: it's a measure of your family's financial strength and ability to pay for college.[24]

Your family's income typically has the most substantial impact on the EFC calculation. This includes both taxed and untaxed income, and it's important to understand that income from both parents and students is considered, though at different weights. Student income is assessed at a higher rate than parent income, which can affect decisions about student employment during the base tax year used for FAFSA calculations.

Assets are another crucial component of the EFC formula, but not all assets are treated equally. Retirement accounts and the equity in your primary residence are protected and not counted in the EFC calculation. However, savings accounts, investments, and additional real estate holdings are included. Understanding these distinctions can help families make informed decisions about where to keep their savings and how to structure their assets.

One of the most significant factors that can affect your EFC is having multiple family members in college simultaneously. The EFC is typically divided by the number of family members attending college, which can substantially reduce each student's individual EFC. For example, if your family's calculated EFC is $20,000 with one child in college, it could potentially drop to $10,000 per child if two children are enrolled at the same time.

To optimize your EFC and potentially increase aid eligibility, consider these strategic approaches:

- Time major income events carefully, avoiding significant capital gains or bonuses during the base tax year used for FAFSA calculations
- Maximize contributions to retirement accounts during the years leading up to college, as these assets are protected
- Consider paying down consumer debt with excessive savings before filing FAFSA, as debt isn't subtracted from assets in the formula, but high savings can increase your EFC
- Plan major necessary purchases before filing the FAFSA to reduce reportable assets

It's crucial to understand that while you can take steps to optimize your EFC, all financial information must be reported accurately and honestly on the FAFSA. The goal is not to manipulate the system but to make informed decisions about timing and asset management that align with both your family's financial needs and the federal aid formula's structure.

Remember that your EFC isn't necessarily what you'll actually pay for college. As noted by financial aid experts, it's simply a number used to determine aid eligibility.[24] Your actual out-of-pocket costs will depend on each school's total cost of attendance, the specific financial aid package offered, and any scholarships or grants received.

When planning for college expenses, start by using the Department of Education's Net Price Calculator to estimate your EFC and potential aid eligibility at different schools. This tool can help you understand how your family's financial situation might affect aid awards and allow you to make more informed decisions about college selection and financing strategies.

By understanding how the EFC is calculated and taking appropriate steps to optimize your family's financial position, you can potentially increase your eligibility for need-based aid[24] and reduce your overall college costs. However, remember that this is just one part of a comprehensive college funding strategy that should also include careful college selection, scholarship applications, and consideration of various educational pathways.

Special Circumstances and Appeals: How to Request Professional Judgment Reviews

Life circumstances can change dramatically after submitting your FAFSA, potentially affecting your ability to pay for college in ways not reflected in your initial application. Understanding how to request a professional judgment review from your school's financial aid office can mean the difference between having to withdraw from college and being able to continue your education when facing unexpected financial challenges.[26-28]

Professional judgment reviews allow financial aid administrators to adjust your FAFSA information when special circumstances arise. These circumstances might include loss of employment, divorce or separation, death of a parent or spouse, extraordinary medical expenses, or other unusual financial hardships that impact your family's ability to pay for college.[26-28]

The first step in requesting a professional judgment review is ensuring you've completed the standard FAFSA process. You must have submitted your FAFSA and received an initial financial aid award before requesting a review. If your application was selected for verification, you'll need to complete that process as well before proceeding with your appeal.[27, 30]

When preparing your appeal, documentation is crucial. Financial aid offices require written evidence of your changed circumstances. For example, if a parent lost their job, you'll need to provide a termination letter and unemployment documentation. For medical expenses, gather copies of bills and proof of payment. For divorce situations, include the divorce decree and documentation showing separate addresses. The more thoroughly you can document your situation, the stronger your appeal will be.[27, 30]

Contact your school's financial aid office directly to understand their specific process for professional judgment reviews. Each institution may have different forms and procedures, but all will require a written appeal explaining your circumstances and how they affect your ability to pay for college. Many schools now use online portals for submitting appeals and supporting documentation securely.[26, 27, 29]

Timing is important when submitting your appeal. While you can request a review at any point during the academic year, you must submit all documentation before the end of the term or year for which you're seeking aid adjustments. To avoid processing delays that could affect your aid, aim to submit your appeal at least three weeks before the semester ends.[30]

Remember that professional judgment reviews are conducted on a case-by-case basis, and approval isn't guaranteed. Even if your appeal is approved, it may not necessarily result in increased financial aid. However, working closely with your financial aid office and providing complete, accurate information gives you the best chance of receiving a fair review that reflects your current financial reality.[30]

When communicating with the financial aid office, maintain a professional approach. Keep copies of all submitted documents, follow up regularly on your appeal's status, and respond promptly to any requests for additional information. Most schools will notify you of their decision through your student email account within two to four weeks of receiving your complete appeal package.[27, 30]

If your appeal is approved, the financial aid office will recalculate your aid eligibility based on your updated circumstances. This could result in changes to your Expected Family Contribution (EFC) and potentially lead to increased grant aid or access to additional loan options. If your appeal is denied, you'll retain your original aid package, but you may be able to explore other financing options with the financial aid office.[30]

Protect your personal information throughout the appeal process. Never email sensitive documents like tax returns or W-2s directly. Instead, use your school's secure document upload system or submit papers in person or by mail as directed by your financial aid office. This ensures your private financial information remains secure while being properly reviewed for your appeal.[30] As we conclude our exploration of the FAFSA process, remember that this vital form serves as your gateway to billions of dollars in available financial aid.

Throughout my years as a counselor, I've seen countless families transform their college funding outlook through careful attention to FAFSA submission and strategic financial planning. The Thompson family's story reminds us that understanding how to properly report assets and income can significantly impact aid eligibility, potentially unlocking thousands in additional funding.

The key lessons from this chapter emphasize several critical points about the FAFSA process. First, timing matters - submitting your FAFSA early can give you access to more aid opportunities, as some funding is distributed on a first-come, first-served basis. Second, accuracy is crucial - take time to gather all necessary documentation and understand how to report your information correctly. Third, don't hesitate to seek professional guidance or request a review if your circumstances change - financial aid offices are there to help you navigate this process.

Remember that the FAFSA isn't just a one-time task but an annual opportunity to secure funding for your education. Each year brings a chance to reassess your situation and potentially qualify for additional aid. Whether you're dealing with basic income reporting or complex situations involving business assets or special circumstances, approaching the FAFSA with knowledge and preparation can make a significant difference in your college funding outcomes.

As you move forward with your college planning journey, keep this chapter's tools and strategies in mind. Document gathering, deadline tracking, and understanding how to optimize your Expected Family Contribution are all crucial skills that will serve you well throughout your college years. The FAFSA may seem daunting at first, but with proper preparation and understanding, it becomes a manageable and essential step toward making college more affordable.

For families still uncertain about the process, remember that help is available. School counselors, college financial aid offices, and online resources can provide additional guidance and support. The most important step is to commit to completing the FAFSA each year, regardless of your financial situation. You might be surprised by the aid opportunities available to you, and you'll never know unless you apply.

Chapter 4:

Beyond Traditional Paths: Alternative Routes to Affordable Education

The path to higher education isn't a one-size-fits-all journey, and some of the most cost-effective routes often go unexplored by families focused solely on traditional four-year colleges. As both a counselor and parent, I've witnessed countless students achieve their educational goals while minimizing debt through alternative pathways that many overlook. While traditional four-year universities remain an excellent path for many students, the evolving landscape of higher education offers numerous alternative routes that can significantly reduce the cost of earning a degree. These paths, from community college transfer programs to military service opportunities, often provide unique advantages beyond just financial savings, including flexible scheduling, practical work experience, and specialized training opportunities.

I've seen firsthand how exploring these alternative pathways can transform seemingly impossible college dreams into achievable realities. Early in my counseling career, I worked with a student named Alex who was determined to become an engineer but was concerned about the cost of a four-year engineering program. Instead of immediately enrolling in a university, we developed a strategic plan using our state's guaranteed transfer program. Alex completed two years at our local community college, maintaining a 3.8 GPA while working part-time. The total cost for these two years was $12,000, compared to the $45,000 it would have cost at the state university. Alex then transferred seamlessly to the university's engineering program, where his strong academic performance earned him merit scholarships for his remaining two years. By graduation, Alex had saved over $40,000 and secured a position at a leading engineering firm. His success story became a powerful example that I share with other students about how alternative pathways can lead to the same destination with significantly less debt. The key was careful planning, understanding transfer agreements, and maintaining academic excellence throughout the journey.

In this chapter, we'll explore various alternative paths to earning a college degree, including community college transfer programs, military education benefits, online degree options, and trade school opportunities. We'll examine how each option works, its potential cost savings, and the important factors to consider when deciding if an alternative path might be right for you. Most importantly, we'll look at how to evaluate these options in the context of your career goals and financial circumstances.

Whether you're considering military service, exploring community college options, or investigating online degree programs, understanding these alternatives can open doors to affordable education you might not have thought possible. The key is to approach these options with thorough research and careful planning, ensuring that the path you choose aligns with both your academic goals and financial realities.

Community College Transfer Programs: Strategic Pathways to Bachelor's Degrees

Community college transfer programs represent one of the most strategic and cost-effective pathways to earning a bachelor's degree. These programs allow students to complete their first two years of college at significantly reduced tuition rates before transferring to a four-year institution to complete their degree. With careful planning and understanding of transfer agreements, students can save tens of thousands of dollars while still achieving their educational goals.[34]

The financial advantages of this pathway are substantial and quantifiable. Community college tuition rates typically run 60-70% lower than four-year institutions for the same foundational courses. For example, completing two years of general education requirements at a community college often costs between $6,000 - $8,000 in tuition, compared to $20,000 - $30,000 at many four-year universities. This difference alone can reduce the total cost of a bachelor's degree by $12,000 - $22,000 before additional savings from lower room and board costs are even considered.[34, 33]

To maximize the benefits of transfer programs, students should focus on three key strategies. First, work closely with transfer counselors at both institutions to ensure all credits will transfer successfully.[32] Second, complete an associate degree before transferring, as research shows this increases both credit acceptance and academic success at the four-year institution.[33] Third, carefully review and understand transfer agreements between specific institutions, including core-to-core agreements that guarantee general education requirements will be satisfied.[33]

Transfer agreements between community colleges and four-year universities come in several forms, each offering distinct advantages. Core-to-core agreements ensure that completing an associate degree satisfies all general education requirements at the partner four-year school. Program-to-program agreements match specific associate degrees with bachelor's degree programs, guaranteeing that all credits apply directly to the intended major. Some institutions even offer dual admission agreements, allowing students to be conditionally admitted to both schools simultaneously.[33]

However, successful transfer requires careful attention to detail and advanced planning. Students must maintain minimum grade requirements, typically a C or better, for courses to transfer.[31] They should also verify that their chosen courses align with their intended major at the four-year institution, as some programs, particularly in STEM fields, may have specific prerequisites that must be completed either before or after transfer.[32]

The academic benefits of starting at a community college extend beyond cost savings. Smaller class sizes and more individualized attention from instructors can help students build a strong academic foundation. Additionally, community colleges often provide extensive support services, including dedicated transfer counselors, academic planning resources, and tutoring programs, all designed to help students succeed in their transition to a four-year institution.[32]

When evaluating potential transfer pathways, students should utilize online tools and resources provided by both institutions to map out their academic journey. Many states maintain comprehensive transfer databases that allow students to see exactly how their community college courses will transfer to different four-year institutions.[32] This advance planning helps avoid taking unnecessary courses and ensures the most efficient path to a bachelor's degree.

The key to successful transfer lies in early planning and regular communication with academic advisors at both institutions. Students should begin researching transfer options and requirements as soon as they start their community college journey, ensuring they understand exactly what courses and grades they need to achieve their goals.[31, 32] This proactive approach helps avoid common pitfalls like non-transferable credits or missing prerequisites that could delay graduation.

While the transfer pathway requires careful planning and dedication, the financial and academic benefits make it an increasingly attractive option for many students. By combining the cost savings of community college with the resources and opportunities available at four-year institutions, transfer programs offer a strategic solution to the challenge of financing higher education while maintaining academic quality and career preparation.[34, 33]

Military Education Benefits: Understanding GI Bill and Service Academy Options

Military education benefits represent one of the most comprehensive pathways to debt-free higher education, offering opportunities through both the GI Bill and service academies. These programs can cover not only tuition but also provide additional benefits like housing allowances and book stipends, making them powerful tools for families planning their education funding strategy.

The Post-9/11 GI Bill, the most substantial education benefit currently available to service members,[35] provides remarkable coverage for those who qualify. For eligible veterans, the program covers full tuition and fees at public schools for in-state students, along with a monthly housing allowance and up to $1,000 annually for books and supplies.[36] At private institutions, the program provides significant support up to an annual maximum amount. The benefit period extends to 36 months of full-time education,[36] effectively covering a four-year degree program.

Qualification for these benefits requires careful planning and understanding of service requirements. Veterans need at least 90 days of active duty service to receive partial benefits, with full benefits typically requiring three years of service.[37] The benefits increase proportionally with length of service,[37] making it essential to understand these thresholds when planning a military education path.

One particularly valuable aspect of the Post-9/11 GI Bill is the ability to transfer unused education benefits to spouses or children.[36] This transferability feature can become a crucial part of family education planning, essentially providing a pathway for family members to obtain affordable higher education. However, this option requires careful, advanced planning as service members must make transfer decisions while still on active duty.

For students considering a more direct path to combining military service with education, service academies offer another compelling option. Institutions like West Point, the Naval Academy, and the Air Force Academy provide full four-year scholarships that cover tuition, room, board, and medical care. These programs essentially offer a debt-free education in exchange for a service commitment, typically five years of active duty following graduation.

The Montgomery GI Bill offers an alternative structure, combining service members' own contributions with government funding to help pay for education benefits.[37] Unlike the Post-9/11 version, these benefits must be used within ten years of completing military service,[37] making timing a crucial consideration in education planning. Recipients receive monthly payments that vary based on course load rather than direct tuition payments to institutions.[36]

When evaluating military education benefits as a pathway to affordable higher education, families should consider several key factors. First, assess the length and type of military service they're willing to commit to, understanding that different service periods qualify for different benefit levels. Second, compare the various GI Bill programs to determine which best aligns with their educational goals. Third, consider whether the structured environment of a service academy or the flexibility of choosing their own institution with GI Bill benefits better suits their needs.

The range of educational pursuits covered by these benefits extends far beyond traditional college programs. The GI Bill can be applied to college and university tuition, online and part-time schooling, licensing and certification courses, vocational training, trade schools, entrepreneurship training, and even flight school.[37] This flexibility allows service members and veterans to pursue various educational paths aligned with their career goals.

For families exploring military education benefits, early planning is crucial. Understanding the requirements, timelines, and commitments involved can help make informed decisions about whether this path aligns with their educational and career goals. Whether through direct service, service academies, or benefit transfers to family members, military education benefits provide powerful options for achieving higher education goals while minimizing or eliminating student debt.

Online and Hybrid Programs: Balancing Quality, Flexibility, and Cost

The landscape of higher education has dramatically evolved, with online and hybrid programs emerging as increasingly viable pathways to earning a degree while potentially reducing costs. These programs combine the flexibility of remote learning with varying levels of in-person instruction, offering students alternatives to traditional campus-based education that can significantly impact both educational quality and affordability.

The financial implications of choosing an online or hybrid program can be substantial. Students often save considerably on living expenses by studying from home, eliminating or reducing costs for campus housing and transportation. Some online programs, particularly at public institutions, offer reduced tuition rates compared to their on-campus counterparts.[41] However, it's crucial to consider the total cost of attendance, including technology fees, required equipment, and learning materials, as these can impact the overall affordability of the program.[39]

Quality considerations should be at the forefront of any decision to pursue online or hybrid education. Accreditation serves as a critical indicator of program quality and should be a non-negotiable factor in program selection.[42] Students should specifically look for regional accreditation, which is generally considered the gold standard for academic programs. The distinction between for-profit and non-profit institutions is particularly important in the online education space, as research has shown that for-profit online colleges often have lower graduation rates and higher student debt burdens compared to their non-profit counterparts.[40]

Flexibility represents one of the most significant advantages of online and hybrid programs, particularly for students balancing work, family, or other commitments.[40] These programs can be especially valuable for students in rural or underserved areas who might otherwise lack access to certain educational opportunities.[42] The ability to complete coursework on a more flexible schedule allows many students to maintain employment while studying, potentially reducing the need for student loans.[40]

However, success in online and hybrid programs requires careful consideration of personal learning styles and technological requirements. Students must have reliable internet access and appropriate technology to participate effectively.[41] Additionally, these programs often demand strong self-motivation and time management skills, as the independent nature of online learning can be challenging for some students.[40]

When evaluating online and hybrid programs, prospective students should consider several key factors:

- Program Accreditation and Reputation
- Total Cost of Attendance (including technology fees and required equipment)
- Available Student Support Services
- Graduate Outcomes and Employment Rates
- Technology Requirements and Support
- Opportunities for Interaction with Faculty and Peers

The COVID-19 pandemic has accelerated the adoption and acceptance of online and hybrid education formats, leading many traditional institutions to expand their digital offerings.[38] This expansion has created more options for students seeking flexible, affordable pathways to degrees. However, it has also made it more important than ever to carefully evaluate program quality and fit.

For families considering online or hybrid programs as a cost-saving strategy, early planning and thorough research are essential. Start by investigating programs at reputable, non-profit institutions that offer strong student support services and clear paths to degree completion.[40] Compare the total cost of attendance between online and traditional programs, factoring in all associated expenses. Consider beginning with a hybrid program that combines the cost benefits of online learning with some in-person instruction,[42] particularly for students who may be uncertain about fully online education.

The key to success in online and hybrid programs lies in matching the program format with individual learning styles, technological capabilities, and career goals. While these alternative pathways can offer significant cost savings and flexibility, they require careful evaluation to ensure they provide the quality education and career preparation students need for long-term success. As we conclude our exploration of alternative pathways to higher education, it's clear that the traditional four-year university route is just one of many viable paths to achieving your educational goals. The stories and strategies we've examined in this chapter demonstrate how thinking creatively about your educational journey can lead to significant cost savings while maintaining the quality of your education.

Whether through community college transfer programs that can save upwards of $40,000 in total costs, military education benefits that can fully fund your degree, or online programs that allow you to maintain employment while studying, these alternative paths offer powerful solutions to the challenge of college affordability. The key lies not in choosing the most obvious path, but in selecting the route that best aligns with your unique circumstances, career goals, and financial resources.

From Alex's successful journey through the community college transfer program to the comprehensive benefits available through military service, we've seen how careful planning and strategic thinking can transform seemingly unattainable educational goals into achievable realities. These paths require thorough research and dedication, but the potential rewards, both financial and personal, make them worthy of serious consideration.

For families exploring different educational pathways, remember that the most important factors are understanding your options, planning early, and carefully evaluating how each path aligns with your long-term goals. Consider starting with these key questions:

- How do different educational paths align with your career goals?
- What are the total costs associated with each option?
- What support systems and resources are available?
- How will different paths impact your long-term financial health?

The landscape of higher education continues to evolve, offering more flexibility and options than ever before. Whether you choose a traditional university experience, pursue a community college transfer program, serve in the military, or explore online education, success comes from matching your chosen path with your individual needs and circumstances.

Remember that there's no one 'right' way to pursue higher education. The best path is the one that leads to your educational goals while minimizing debt and maximizing opportunities for future success. By understanding and carefully evaluating these alternative pathways, you can make informed decisions that support both your academic ambitions and financial well-being.

As we move forward, keep in mind that the strategies and paths we've discussed in this chapter can be combined and customized to create your own unique route to an affordable education. The key is to remain flexible, informed, and focused on your ultimate educational and career goals while being strategic about the financial implications of your choices.

Chapter 5:

The Scholarship Success Blueprint: Finding and Winning Hidden Opportunities

While most students focus their scholarship search on well-known national awards, the real treasure trove of college funding often lies hidden in plain sight within local communities, professional organizations, and niche interest groups. Understanding how to uncover and successfully compete for these lesser-known opportunities can be the difference between modest aid and substantial scholarship funding. The scholarship landscape is vast and varied, with countless opportunities that extend far beyond academic excellence or athletic achievement. While national scholarships often garner the most attention, they also face the fiercest competition, making it crucial to develop a comprehensive strategy that encompasses both high-profile and lesser-known opportunities.

I've witnessed firsthand how a strategic approach to scholarship hunting can transform seemingly modest opportunities into substantial funding. Local organizations, professional associations, and community groups often offer scholarships that receive surprisingly few applications, creating golden opportunities for prepared students who take the time to seek them out.

During my second year as a high school counselor, I worked with a student named Emma who was determined to fund her education primarily through scholarships but had limited success with major national awards. Together, we developed a systematic approach focusing on local opportunities. Emma created a spreadsheet to track application deadlines and requirements, then researched every local business, community organization, and professional association in our area. She discovered that our local credit union offered three $2,500 scholarships that typically received fewer than 20 applications each year. The town's garden club had a $1,500 scholarship that hadn't been awarded the previous year due to a lack of applicants. Emma applied for 45 local scholarships in total, many with minimal competition. Her systematic approach and well-crafted essays, which we refined for each application, helped her win 12 scholarships totaling $22,000. The key to her success wasn't just finding the opportunities but understanding how to tailor her applications to each organization's mission and values.

Emma's story exemplifies a fundamental truth about scholarship success: it's not always the biggest awards that make the most significant impact. Rather, it's the cumulative effect of multiple smaller awards, strategically pursued and carefully managed, that can create a substantial funding package. Her experience shows that with organization, persistence, and a willingness to explore every avenue, students can build impressive scholarship portfolios that significantly reduce or eliminate the need for student loans.

In this chapter, we'll explore proven strategies for uncovering these hidden scholarship opportunities, developing compelling applications, and managing the scholarship search process efficiently. You'll learn how to craft standout essays, build strong relationships with recommenders, and maintain the organization necessary to submit multiple high-quality applications while balancing academic responsibilities. We'll also examine how to leverage your unique interests, experiences, and affiliations to find scholarships that align with your personal story and aspirations.

Local and Niche Scholarship Mining: Finding Hidden Gems in Your Community

One of the most effective strategies for reducing college costs lies in systematically exploring and applying for local and niche scholarships that many students overlook. These opportunities, often offered by community organizations, local businesses, and special interest groups, typically have far less competition than national scholarships[44] while still providing substantial funding potential.

Local scholarship hunting begins with a thorough exploration of your immediate community. Start by creating a comprehensive list of potential funding sources, including:

- Local businesses and corporations
- Community foundations and charitable organizations
- Religious institutions
- Professional associations and trade groups
- Civic organizations (Rotary, Lions Club, etc.)
- Chamber of Commerce
- Credit unions and local banks

These local opportunities often have unique advantages that make them particularly valuable for strategic scholarship seekers. First, the applicant pool is naturally limited by geographic restrictions, significantly increasing your chances of success.[44] Second, many local scholarships go unclaimed each year simply because students aren't aware they exist.[44] For instance, community foundations often manage multiple scholarship funds,[45] with some receiving fewer than 20 applications for awards ranging from $500 to $2,500.

To maximize your success with local scholarships, develop a systematic approach to identifying and tracking opportunities. Create a detailed spreadsheet or digital document that includes application deadlines, requirements, and award amounts. Pay particular attention to documentation requirements; many local scholarships require specific elements like letters of recommendation from community members or proof of local residency.[45]

Niche scholarships represent another valuable category of often-overlooked funding opportunities. These awards target students with specific characteristics, interests, or career goals.[43] The key to success with niche scholarships is identifying those that align with your unique attributes and experiences. Consider scholarships related to:

- Academic interests or intended major
- Cultural or ethnic background
- Special talents or hobbies
- Family circumstances or characteristics
- Career aspirations
- Community service focus

When applying for both local and niche scholarships, it's crucial to tailor your applications to each organization's specific mission and values. Research the sponsoring organization thoroughly and align your application materials with their goals and priorities. For example, if applying for a scholarship from a local environmental organization, emphasize any relevant volunteer work or environmental interests in your application.

Timing is also critical in the scholarship search process. While many students wait until senior year to begin applying, the most successful scholarship seekers start their search during junior year or earlier.[43] This early start allows time to develop strong relationships with potential recommenders, craft compelling essays, and meet early deadlines for some of the most prestigious opportunities.

Remember that even smaller scholarship awards can add up significantly.[43] A strategic approach might involve applying for multiple local and niche scholarships rather than focusing solely on highly competitive national awards. For instance, winning five local scholarships worth $1,000 each could match or exceed a single national award, with potentially less competition for each opportunity.

To maintain organization throughout the process, consider creating a monthly scholarship calendar that includes:

- Application deadlines
- Required materials and documentation
- Follow-up dates for recommendations
- Interview schedules (if applicable)
- Notification dates

This systematic approach to local and niche scholarship hunting can significantly impact your overall college funding strategy. By dedicating time to thoroughly researching and pursuing these opportunities, you can build a substantial scholarship portfolio while developing valuable skills in professional communication and application preparation.

Application Excellence: Crafting Compelling Essays and Building Strong Portfolios

The scholarship essay and portfolio represent your opportunity to stand out among thousands of applicants, making the difference between securing vital funding and missing out on crucial financial aid. While many students focus solely on listing achievements, the most successful scholarship applications tell compelling stories that demonstrate character, resilience, and potential impact.

Crafting an effective scholarship essay begins with authentic storytelling that reveals who you are beyond grades and test scores. Rather than simply stating accomplishments, successful applicants weave narratives that demonstrate how their experiences have shaped their goals and values. This approach helps scholarship committees connect with applicants on a personal level and understand their potential impact on campus and beyond.

A well-structured scholarship essay maintains a clear focus throughout while addressing the prompt directly. Start with a captivating hook that draws readers in, maintain a coherent narrative structure, and conclude with a meaningful reflection that ties back to your future goals. Remember that scholarship committees often read hundreds or thousands of essays; your opening paragraph must immediately engage their interest while remaining authentic to your voice.

The editing process is crucial for developing compelling scholarship essays. Allow time between writing and editing sessions to gain a fresh perspective on your work. Seek feedback from teachers, mentors, and peers who can provide constructive criticism. Reading essays aloud helps catch awkward phrasing and ensures your authentic voice shines through. Most importantly, eliminate unnecessary words while preserving the impact of your narrative.

Building a strong scholarship portfolio requires comprehensive but selective documentation of your achievements. Beyond basic academic accomplishments, include evidence of leadership roles and their measurable impact, community service activities, and special projects you've initiated or led. The goal is to demonstrate a trajectory of growth rather than simply listing static achievements. Scholarship committees value seeing how students have progressed and overcome obstacles.

One of the most common mistakes students make is using generic materials for all scholarship applications. Successful applicants research each scholarship's mission, values, and specific evaluation criteria. Your application should be tailored to align with these elements while maintaining authenticity. This means understanding the organization's goals and demonstrating how your experiences and aspirations match their priorities.

When building your portfolio, consider both traditional and digital formats, as many scholarships now accept or require digital submissions. Ensure your materials are professional in presentation, easy to navigate, and consistent in formatting. Remember that selective presentation is often more effective than exhaustive documentation; choose materials that tell a compelling story about your journey and potential.

Don't overlook the importance of strong recommendation letters in your scholarship applications. Request letters well in advance of deadlines and provide recommenders with relevant information about your achievements and the scholarship's focus. Suggest specific points they might address that align with the scholarship criteria, and always follow up with thank-you notes regardless of the outcome.

To manage the scholarship application process effectively, create a sustainable system for tracking deadlines and organizing materials. Dedicate specific weekly time blocks to scholarship applications, breaking the process into manageable components. Develop a master resume documenting all activities and achievements, along with several core essays addressing common themes that can be customized for specific applications.

Remember that smaller scholarships often have less competition while still providing valuable funding. Many students focus exclusively on large, competitive awards while ignoring smaller opportunities that could add up significantly.[16] Create a detailed calendar of application deadlines and work backward to establish timelines for completing each component, ensuring you don't miss out on any opportunities due to poor planning.

The scholarship application process requires dedication, authenticity, and strategic thinking.[6] By developing compelling essays and strong portfolios that genuinely reflect your experiences and aspirations, you significantly increase your chances of securing the funding needed to pursue higher education without crushing debt. Treat the application process as a part-time job, investing the time and effort needed to create materials that showcase your unique qualities and potential.[6]

Scholarship Management Systems: Organizing Applications and Maximizing Success Rates

In today's digital age, successful scholarship applicants understand that organization and systematic management of applications can dramatically increase their chances of securing funding. A well-structured scholarship management system serves as the foundation for maximizing application success rates while efficiently handling multiple submissions, deadlines, and requirements.

Modern scholarship management has evolved significantly from paper-based tracking to sophisticated digital platforms that streamline the entire process. These systems help students centralize their scholarship search, application materials, and deadline tracking in one accessible location. Leading platforms like SmarterSelect,[46] Good Grants,[47] and Blackbaud Award Management[46] offer comprehensive solutions that can transform a scattered approach into a strategic campaign for college funding.

The key to maximizing scholarship success begins with creating a robust digital organization system. Start by establishing a master spreadsheet or utilizing specialized scholarship management software to track:

- Scholarship names and award amounts
- Application deadlines and requirements
- Essay prompts and word counts
- Required documentation and recommendations
- Submission status and follow-up dates

AI-powered platforms like ScholarshipOwl have revolutionized the scholarship application process by providing personalized scholarship recommendations based on user profiles and application habits.[48] These advanced systems can analyze your profile and suggest scholarships that align with your specific qualifications, significantly increasing your chances of success while reducing time spent searching for opportunities.

One of the most powerful features of modern scholarship management systems is their ability to help students repurpose application materials efficiently. Rather than creating entirely new essays for each application, these platforms help identify opportunities to adapt existing materials,[48] allowing students to apply for more scholarships without proportionally increasing their workload.

Real-time tracking capabilities have become essential for serious scholarship applicants. Modern platforms enable students to monitor application statuses, upcoming deadlines, and required follow-up actions in real-time.[48] This visibility helps ensure no opportunities are missed while maintaining a consistent application pace throughout the scholarship season.

To maximize success rates, focus on creating comprehensive profiles within your chosen management system. These detailed profiles should highlight your unique qualifications, achievements, and circumstances, improving the matching algorithms' effectiveness in connecting you with relevant opportunities. The most successful applicants use these systems to target scholarships where they have the strongest competitive advantage, rather than applying indiscriminately.

When selecting a scholarship management system, consider platforms that offer:

- Automated scholarship matching
- Deadline reminder systems
- Document storage and organization
- Essay template management
- Application status tracking
- Recommendation letter management

The future of scholarship management continues to evolve with more sophisticated AI capabilities and predictive analytics. These innovations are making it easier for students to identify and secure funding opportunities that align with their specific circumstances and goals. By leveraging these tools effectively, students can significantly improve their chances of securing substantial scholarship funding for their education.

Remember that successful scholarship management isn't just about tracking applications; it's about creating a sustainable system that allows you to maintain quality while increasing the quantity of your applications. Set aside dedicated time each week for scholarship activities, using your management system to prioritize applications based on deadlines, award amounts, and alignment with your qualifications.

As you develop your scholarship management strategy, focus on quality matches rather than quantity alone. Use your system to identify opportunities where your unique strengths and experiences align closely with the scholarship's mission and criteria. This targeted approach, combined with efficient organization and tracking, can significantly improve your success rate in securing college funding. As we conclude our exploration of scholarship strategies, it's crucial to remember that success in securing college funding rarely comes from a single large award. Rather, it's the cumulative impact of a well-executed, multi-faceted approach that combines local opportunities, niche scholarships, and strategic application management. The stories of students like Emma, who secured $22,000 through multiple local scholarships, demonstrate how persistence and organization can transform seemingly modest opportunities into substantial funding packages.

The scholarship landscape may seem overwhelming at first, but breaking it down into manageable components, from local scholarship mining to portfolio development and application management, creates a clear path forward. Remember that every scholarship application is an opportunity not just to secure funding, but to refine your story, develop your professional communication skills, and clarify your educational goals.

As both a counselor and parent, I've witnessed how students who approach the scholarship process systematically, starting their search early and maintaining consistent effort throughout their senior year, typically achieve the best results. They understand that scholarship success isn't about luck; it's about preparation, perseverance, and strategic thinking. Whether you're targeting local community awards, pursuing niche opportunities aligned with your unique interests, or applying for traditional merit-based scholarships, the principles of thorough research, compelling storytelling, and meticulous organization remain constant.

Moving forward, commit to treating your scholarship search as a part-time job. Set aside dedicated time each week for research, writing, and application management. Build strong relationships with teachers and community members who can provide powerful letters of recommendation. Most importantly, don't let rejections discourage you; every application is an opportunity to improve your approach and move closer to your funding goals.

Remember that the strategies outlined in this chapter, from creating comprehensive application tracking systems to crafting compelling personal narratives, are proven approaches that have helped countless students secure substantial scholarship funding. By implementing these techniques consistently and maintaining focus on your goals, you can significantly reduce the financial burden of your college education while developing valuable skills that will serve you well throughout your academic and professional career.

As you begin your own scholarship journey, stay focused on the end goal: making college affordable without crushing debt. Every hour invested in scholarship applications has the potential to save thousands in future loan payments. With dedication, organization, and strategic thinking, you can build a scholarship portfolio that transforms your college funding outlook and puts you on the path to achieving your educational dreams without the weight of excessive student loans.

Chapter 6:

Smart College Selection: Balancing Program Quality with Cost

Selecting the right college involves far more than choosing between dream schools and safety schools; it requires a careful analysis of both program quality and financial impact on your family's future. The most expensive college isn't necessarily the best choice, nor is the cheapest option always the wisest path to your career goals. When families focus solely on college rankings or campus amenities, they often overlook the critical relationship between program quality and long-term financial outcomes. As someone who has guided hundreds of families through this decision process, I've witnessed firsthand how choosing the right academic program at the right price point can set students up for future success, or burden them with unnecessary debt.

In my role as a high school counselor, I worked with a talented student named Rachel who was torn between an expensive private university and a more affordable state school for her intended major in computer science. The private university had offered her a $20,000 annual scholarship, but it would still cost $35,000 per year after aid. The state university's total cost would be $22,000 annually. Together, we researched both programs extensively, comparing their curriculum requirements, internship opportunities, and job placement rates. We discovered that while both programs were accredited and well-regarded, the state university had stronger industry partnerships in our region and similar job placement rates to the private school.

Rachel's family calculated that choosing the state university would save them $52,000 over four years. They decided to invest a small portion of these savings in professional certifications and summer coding bootcamps to enhance Rachel's resume. By graduation, Rachel had secured a competitive job offer with a starting salary that allowed her to comfortably manage her modest student loans. Her story illustrates how thoughtful analysis of both program quality and cost can lead to financially sound decisions without sacrificing educational outcomes.

This chapter will guide you through the complex process of evaluating colleges based on both academic merit and financial feasibility. We'll explore how to look beyond the surface-level appeal of prestigious names and beautiful campuses to understand the true value proposition of each institution. You'll learn concrete strategies for comparing program offerings, analyzing career outcomes, and calculating the real cost of attendance, not just the sticker price.

More importantly, we'll examine how to align your college choice with your career goals and financial resources. Whether you're considering a liberal arts college, technical institute, or state university, understanding how to evaluate the return on investment for your specific situation is crucial. We'll look at factors like graduation rates, job placement statistics, and starting salaries by major to help you make an informed decision that balances educational quality with financial responsibility.

Remember, the goal isn't to simply find the cheapest option available; it's to identify the best value for your educational investment. Through real examples and practical exercises, you'll develop the tools needed to make this critical decision with confidence and clarity.

Evaluating Program Quality: Rankings, Accreditation, and Career Outcomes

When evaluating college programs, three critical factors deserve careful attention: accreditation status, program rankings, and career outcomes. These elements work together to provide a comprehensive picture of program quality and potential return on investment. Understanding each component helps families make informed decisions that balance educational quality with financial responsibility.

Accreditation serves as the foundation of program quality assessment. This formal review process, conducted by recognized authorities, ensures that colleges meet established standards of academic excellence. Regional accreditation, the most widely recognized type, typically applies to non-profit, degree-granting institutions. National accreditation often covers vocational, technical, or for-profit schools. The distinction is crucial because credits from nationally accredited schools may not transfer to regionally accredited institutions. Always verify a program's accreditation status through the U.S. Department of Education or the Council for Higher Education Accreditation to ensure your investment will be recognized by employers and other institutions.

While college rankings can provide useful comparative insights, they should be viewed as just one piece of the evaluation puzzle. Rankings typically consider factors such as academic reputation, student selectivity, faculty resources, and graduation rates. However, these broad institutional measures may not reflect the quality of specific programs within a university. When examining rankings, focus on program-specific indicators like student-to-faculty ratios, graduation rates, and research opportunities that directly impact your educational experience.[52]

Career outcomes offer perhaps the most concrete measure of program value. Look for data on employment rates in the field of study, median starting salaries, and graduate school placement rates. For programs leading to regulated professions, such as nursing or engineering, pay special attention to licensure exam pass rates.[49, 53] These metrics provide tangible evidence of how well a program prepares students for their chosen careers.

Beyond these primary factors, consider additional quality indicators that can impact your educational experience. Student success metrics like retention rates and course completion rates offer insights into how well a program supports its students.[49, 51] The percentage of faculty with advanced degrees and the availability of research opportunities can indicate the depth of expertise and hands-on learning available to students.[52]

When comparing programs, develop a systematic approach to evaluation. Create a spreadsheet tracking key metrics for each program under consideration. Include both quality indicators and cost factors to develop a clear picture of value.[50, 53] For example, a program with strong career outcomes and high licensure exam pass rates might justify a higher tuition cost compared to a less expensive program with weaker outcomes.

Remember that program quality extends beyond the classroom. Look for evidence of strong industry partnerships, internship programs, and career services support. These elements can significantly impact your ability to transition from education to employment.[50] Some programs maintain advisory boards with industry professionals who help ensure curriculum relevance and create networking opportunities for students.

Finally, don't overlook the importance of program-specific accreditation in certain fields. Professional organizations often accredit individual programs within their disciplines. For instance, engineering programs should have ABET accreditation, while business programs might seek AACSB accreditation. These specialized credentials can affect your ability to secure certain positions or pursue advanced degrees in your field.

By carefully evaluating these various aspects of program quality, you can make an informed decision that balances academic excellence with financial feasibility. Remember that the highest-ranked or most expensive program isn't always the best choice; the key is finding the program that offers the strongest preparation for your career goals at a cost you can manage.

Understanding True Costs: Beyond Tuition to Total Cost of Attendance

When families evaluate college costs, they often focus primarily on tuition rates, creating a dangerous blind spot in their financial planning. The true cost of attending college extends far beyond the basic tuition price tag, encompassing a wide range of expenses that can significantly impact your total investment in higher education.

Understanding these comprehensive costs is crucial for making informed decisions about college affordability and developing realistic financial plans.[55]

Let's break down the actual components of college costs. Direct costs paid to the institution include not just tuition, but also mandatory fees for student activities, health services, technology, and facilities. For example, at many institutions, these mandatory fees can add several thousand dollars annually to your bill. Room and board represents another substantial direct cost, with housing at many private universities costing between $10,000-$12,000 annually, while meal plans can add another $8,000-$9,000 to your yearly expenses.[56]

Indirect costs, though not paid directly to the college, are equally important in your financial planning. Books and supplies alone average $1,220 annually at public 4-year institutions.[54] Personal expenses, transportation, and health insurance can add thousands more to your annual costs. These indirect expenses often catch families off guard because they're not included in the initial tuition bill, but are essential for student success and well-being.

To understand the magnitude of total costs, consider that the average comprehensive cost of attendance at any 4-year institution reaches approximately $38,270 per year, potentially totaling $153,000 over four years.[57] At private institutions, these costs can be substantially higher, with some elite universities posting total annual costs exceeding $90,000 for on-campus students.[56]

When evaluating college costs, it's crucial to consider several often-overlooked factors that can impact your total financial commitment.

First, many students take more than four years to complete their degrees, potentially adding significant costs beyond initial projections. Second, college costs typically increase annually, often at rates exceeding general inflation. Finally, regional variations in living costs can substantially impact your total expenses, particularly if you're considering schools in different parts of the country.

However, it's important to note that the sticker price rarely represents what students actually pay. Financial aid packages can substantially reduce out-of-pocket expenses through a combination of grants, scholarships, and other forms of assistance. Understanding the difference between the published cost of attendance and your net price after financial aid is crucial for making informed decisions about college affordability.[56]

To develop a realistic picture of college costs, create a comprehensive budget that includes all potential expenses. Start by researching the published cost of attendance at your target schools, then break down each component: tuition and fees, room and board, books and supplies, personal expenses, and transportation. Remember to factor in annual increases and potential extended time to graduation. This detailed analysis will help you understand the true financial commitment required and make more informed decisions about college selection and financing strategies.

For example, at public 4-year institutions, tuition represents only about 36% of the total attendance cost for in-state students.[54] This means that even if you've planned for tuition, you still need to account for the remaining 64% of costs that come from other expenses.

Understanding these proportions can help you develop more accurate savings goals and financial plans.

Return on Investment: Analyzing Career Prospects and Starting Salaries by Major

When evaluating college programs, one of the most critical factors to consider is the potential return on investment (ROI); essentially, how your educational investment translates into career opportunities and earning potential. This analysis becomes particularly important as college costs continue to rise and student debt reaches concerning levels across the nation.

STEM fields consistently demonstrate some of the strongest returns on investment. Engineering graduates, particularly those specializing in petroleum, computer, electrical, and chemical engineering, typically enjoy some of the highest employment rates and starting salaries among all bachelor's degree recipients.[58] Computer science and mathematics majors also command impressive starting salaries, often well above the national average for college graduates. These fields continue to grow as industries become increasingly technology-driven, creating a favorable long-term outlook for graduates.

Business and economics majors also tend to see strong returns on their educational investment. Finance, accounting, and business analytics specialists often secure competitive starting salaries and enjoy significant potential for career advancement.[58] Healthcare-related majors, particularly nursing and other medical specialties, demonstrate excellent career prospects due to growing healthcare needs and typically offer strong starting compensation[58].

However, it's crucial to understand that starting salary isn't the only measure of ROI. When evaluating potential majors, consider using the debt-to-income ratio as a practical framework. Financial experts recommend that total student loan debt should not exceed your expected first-year salary.[1, 75] For example, if you're considering a program that will require $80,000 in student loans, but the average starting salary in your chosen field is $45,000, you may need to reconsider either your college choice or major.

Break-even analysis provides another valuable perspective on ROI. This calculation helps determine how long it will take to recoup your educational investment through increased earnings. While STEM graduates often reach this break-even point faster due to higher starting salaries, humanities graduates may take longer but can still achieve positive lifetime returns[58] through career advancement and the development of valuable transferable skills.

When analyzing potential majors and career paths, look beyond just starting salaries to understand the complete picture of career prospects. Research employment rates, career growth trajectories, and the stability of different industries. For instance, while fine arts or social work majors might start with lower compensation, they can lead to fulfilling careers with growth potential over time.[58] Additionally, some fields that start with moderate salaries, such as education (especially STEM education) and communications, often provide stable employment opportunities with reasonable compensation.

To maximize your educational ROI, consider several strategic approaches. First, research institutions that offer strong programs in your chosen field without necessarily carrying premium price tags.

The prestige of an institution often matters less than the quality and relevance of the education received. Second, look for opportunities to minimize your debt burden through community college transfer programs, in-state public universities, or the aggressive pursuit of scholarships and grants.[5, 59]

Accelerated completion can significantly improve your ROI by reducing costs and allowing earlier entry into the workforce. Develop a clear degree plan that allows you to graduate in four years or less, avoiding unnecessary course changes or additions that could extend your time to graduation.[1,75] Each additional semester not only adds direct costs but also delays your entry into the workforce, impacting your lifetime earnings potential.

Remember that the highest-paying major isn't automatically the best choice for everyone. The key is finding the optimal balance between pursuing a fulfilling career path and ensuring financial stability after graduation. Consider your personal interests, abilities, and long-term career goals alongside potential financial returns. A lower-paying field that aligns with your passions and skills might ultimately lead to greater success than a high-paying field where you're less likely to thrive.

By carefully analyzing career prospects, starting salaries, and educational costs, you can make informed decisions that maximize your educational investment while minimizing debt burden. The goal should be finding a career path that provides both personal fulfillment and financial stability, creating a strong foundation for your professional future. As we conclude our exploration of college selection and costs, it's crucial to remember that the most expensive option isn't always the best, nor is the cheapest path necessarily the wisest choice. The key lies in finding the sweet spot where program quality, career outcomes, and financial feasibility intersect with your personal goals and circumstances.

Throughout this chapter, we've examined how to evaluate program quality through accreditation, rankings, and career outcomes. We've delved into understanding true costs beyond just tuition, and we've explored methods for analyzing return on investment through starting salaries and career prospects. These elements form a comprehensive framework for making informed decisions about college selection.

Remember Rachel's story; by choosing the state university over the more expensive private institution, her family saved $52,000 while still securing a quality education that led to excellent career opportunities. Her success came not from choosing the most prestigious name or the lowest price tag, but from carefully evaluating program quality alongside cost and making strategic investments in additional certifications that enhanced her career prospects.

As you begin your own college selection process, keep these key takeaways in mind:

- Look beyond sticker prices to understand the total cost of attendance, including often-overlooked expenses like mandatory fees, books, and living costs
- Evaluate program quality through multiple lenses: accreditation, career outcomes, and specific departmental strengths
- Consider ROI by comparing potential debt levels with realistic starting salaries in your chosen field

- Research program-specific factors like graduation rates, job placement statistics, and industry partnerships
- Remember that prestige doesn't always correlate with better career outcomes or justify significantly higher costs

The college selection process can feel overwhelming, but by focusing on these core elements, program quality, true costs, and return on investment, you can make decisions that support both your educational goals and financial well-being. Take time to research thoroughly, compare options carefully, and consider how each choice aligns with your long-term career aspirations.

In the next chapter, we'll explore how military service and athletic ability can open additional pathways to college funding, providing unique opportunities for those who qualify. But first, take some time to apply the frameworks we've discussed to your own college search. Create a spreadsheet comparing your potential schools across the key metrics we've covered, and start building your own strategic approach to college selection.

Remember, the goal isn't to find the perfect school; it's to find the right match between your educational needs, career goals, and financial resources. By carefully weighing these factors, you can make choices that set you up for both academic and financial success.

Chapter 7:

Military Benefits and Athletic Scholarships: Special Pathways to College Funding

For students willing to commit to service or excel in athletics, two of the most comprehensive pathways to college funding await: military benefits and athletic scholarships. These unique opportunities not only provide substantial financial support but also offer structured paths to personal development, leadership skills, and career advancement. While both paths require careful consideration and planning, let's first explore military education benefits, which can provide comprehensive funding along with valuable career development opportunities. The Post-9/11 GI Bill offers extensive benefits, including full tuition coverage at public universities, housing allowances, and even the possibility of transferring benefits to family members. ROTC programs, available at more than 1,700 colleges nationwide, provide another avenue, offering full tuition scholarships while preparing students for officer roles after graduation.

For those interested in athletic scholarships, opportunities exist across multiple divisions and associations. Beyond the well-known NCAA Division I programs, NCAA Division II and III schools offer various forms of athletic aid. The National Association of Intercollegiate Athletics (NAIA) also provides significant scholarship opportunities, often with less intense competition for spots than NCAA Division I programs. NAIA schools typically offer a combination of athletic and academic scholarships, making them an attractive option for students who excel in both sports and academics.

The key to successfully navigating either path lies in early preparation and understanding program requirements. For military benefits, students must carefully evaluate service commitments, program eligibility requirements, and how these align with their long-term career goals. Athletes need to understand recruitment timelines, eligibility standards, and a realistic assessment of their athletic abilities at different competitive levels.

In my years as a counselor, I've worked with numerous students who have successfully leveraged these opportunities. Take Marcus, for example, who exemplified how careful planning could maximize these special funding pathways. As a talented track athlete who was interested in military service, Marcus enrolled in ROTC at a Division III college where his track abilities helped him stand out in the program. The ROTC scholarship covered his tuition and fees, while his athletic participation opened doors for leadership roles within the ROTC program.

By his senior year, Marcus had earned additional merit-based scholarships through his ROTC performance, maintained strong academic standing, and set several school records in track. His story demonstrates how students can creatively combine different funding pathways to create comprehensive college financing solutions, and I often use his example to show families how thinking beyond traditional scholarship categories can unlock unique opportunities for college funding.

Military Education Benefits: GI Bill, ROTC, and Service Academies

Military education benefits represent one of the most comprehensive pathways to funding higher education, offering opportunities that can completely cover college costs while providing valuable career experience. These programs fall into three main categories: the GI Bill for veterans and service members, ROTC scholarships for students willing to commit to future service, and service academies offering full-ride opportunities with prestigious military careers.

The Post-9/11 GI Bill stands as one of the most generous education benefits available, covering up to 100% of in-state public tuition and fees, plus providing a monthly housing allowance and an annual stipend for books and supplies. Recent expansions have made these benefits even more valuable, with eligible veterans now able to receive up to 48 months of education benefits if they have multiple periods of qualifying service. Additionally, the Yellow Ribbon Program helps cover costs at private or out-of-state institutions that exceed standard GI Bill payments.

For high school students considering military service as a path to college funding, the Reserve Officers' Training Corps (ROTC) offers substantial scholarships at hundreds of colleges nationwide. ROTC scholarships typically cover full tuition and fees, plus provide a monthly stipend for living expenses and book allowances. However, these benefits come with a significant commitment; usually 4-8 years of service as a commissioned officer after graduation. Students must carefully weigh this long-term commitment against the immediate financial benefits.

Service academies represent the most comprehensive but also the most competitive military education pathway. Institutions like West Point, the Naval Academy, and the Air Force Academy provide full tuition, room, board, and expenses for all admitted students. However, admission requires not only exceptional academic achievement but also leadership qualities, physical fitness, and typically a congressional nomination. Graduates commit to at least five years of active duty service as commissioned officers.

Active duty service members can also access Tuition Assistance (TA) while serving, covering up to $250 per credit hour with a maximum of $4,500 per fiscal year. Many service members strategically use TA during active duty, saving their GI Bill benefits for graduate school or transferring them to family members. This approach maximizes the total education benefits available through military service.

When considering military education benefits, timing and planning are crucial. High school students interested in ROTC should begin preparing as early as sophomore year, focusing on academic excellence, physical fitness, and leadership activities. Those considering service academies should start even earlier, typically in freshman year, to build the comprehensive resume required for these highly selective institutions.

It's essential to understand that military education benefits, while generous, come with serious commitments and responsibilities. Students must carefully evaluate their readiness for military service and understand the full scope of their obligations. Families should thoroughly research each option, considering not just the financial benefits but also the career implications and service requirements that accompany these opportunities.

The application processes for these programs require careful attention to detail and often have strict deadlines. ROTC scholarship applications typically open in the summer before senior year, while service academy applications begin even earlier. The GI Bill requires careful documentation of service time and type of discharge, with benefits varying based on length and nature of service.

While military education benefits can provide a debt-free path to college, they require careful consideration of both short-term and long-term implications. Students must be prepared for the rigors of military training alongside their academic studies, understanding that these programs demand high levels of commitment, discipline, and dedication to both their education and their service obligations.

Athletic Scholarship Fundamentals: NCAA Divisions, Recruitment, and Eligibility

Athletic scholarships represent a significant opportunity for talented student-athletes to fund their college education, but the path requires careful planning and realistic expectations. According to NCAA data, less than 2% of high school athletes receive full athletic scholarships to Division I schools, making it crucial for families to understand both the opportunities and limitations of this funding pathway.

The NCAA operates three distinct divisions, each with unique scholarship regulations and eligibility requirements. Division I schools, representing the highest level of collegiate athletics, require student-athletes to maintain a minimum 2.3 GPA in NCAA-approved core courses. These core courses must follow a specific distribution: 16 approved courses, including English, math, natural/physical science, and social science. Importantly, 10 of these core courses must be completed before the seventh semester of high school, with 7 in English, math, or science.

Division II institutions, while still highly competitive, maintain slightly different requirements. Student-athletes must maintain a 2.2 GPA in their core courses and meet yearly academic progress standards, including earning a 2.0 cumulative GPA. Division II schools often offer partial scholarships, allowing programs to spread their scholarship funds across more athletes. This can create opportunities for students who might not qualify for Division I scholarships but still wish to compete at the collegiate level.

Division III schools, while not offering athletic scholarships, often provide attractive financial aid packages for student-athletes through academic scholarships and need-based aid. This can make Division III schools an affordable option for students who want to continue their athletic careers while prioritizing academics.

The National Association of Intercollegiate Athletics (NAIA) offers another pathway for athletic scholarships, often with less intense competition for spots than NCAA Division I programs. NAIA schools can offer full or partial athletic scholarships and typically combine these with academic scholarships. With more flexible eligibility requirements and a strong focus on character and leadership, NAIA schools present valuable opportunities for student-athletes seeking collegiate competition and scholarship support.

The recruitment process typically begins with registration at the NCAA Eligibility Center or NAIA Eligibility Center, ideally by the end of sophomore year in high school. Even students who are undecided about pursuing athletic scholarships should create a complimentary account to obtain their identification number. This early registration ensures students don't miss important deadlines and allows them to track their progress toward meeting eligibility requirements.

A significant recent change in NCAA policy has eliminated standardized test requirements for initial eligibility. This change, implemented in 2023, applies to all students and represents a major shift in how athletic eligibility is determined. However, academic performance in core courses remains crucial, with specific GPA requirements that must be met and maintained.

To maximize opportunities for athletic scholarships, students should develop a comprehensive strategy that includes:

- Maintaining strong academic performance in approved core courses
- Creating highlight videos and athletic resumes
- Attending camps and showcases where college coaches recruit
- Building relationships with high school coaches who can advocate for their abilities
- Researching schools that offer their sport and have scholarship availability

Understanding the realities of athletic scholarships is crucial for effective planning. Most athletic scholarships are partial rather than full-ride offers, making it important to combine athletic scholarships with other funding sources when planning for college costs. Additionally, athletic scholarships typically require annual renewal based on both athletic performance and academic standing.

The recruitment landscape has become increasingly competitive, with many schools using sophisticated scouting and evaluation systems. Students serious about pursuing athletic scholarships should begin preparing as early as the freshman year of high school, focusing on both athletic development and academic achievement. This dual focus ensures they meet eligibility requirements while developing the skills necessary to compete at the collegiate level.

For families considering this pathway, maintaining perspective and developing contingency plans is essential. While athletic scholarships can provide significant financial support, they should be viewed as one component of a broader college funding strategy. Students should continue to pursue academic excellence, apply for other scholarships, and consider alternative funding sources in case athletic scholarship opportunities don't materialize as hoped.

Success in securing athletic scholarships often requires proactive communication with coaches and athletic departments. Students should understand NCAA and NAIA rules regarding contact periods and permissible communications while also maintaining detailed records of their athletic achievements and academic progress. This documentation becomes crucial during the recruitment process and scholarship negotiations.

Maintaining eligibility once in college requires ongoing commitment to both academic and athletic performance. Student-athletes must complete a certain percentage of their degree requirements each year while adhering to amateurism standards throughout their collegiate career. The demands of balancing athletics and academics require strong time management skills and dedication to both aspects of student-athlete life.

Athletic scholarships can significantly reduce college costs for talented student-athletes, but success requires early planning, realistic expectations, and a clear understanding of NCAA and NAIA requirements and recruitment processes. Families should approach this pathway as one part of a comprehensive college funding strategy, always maintaining focus on both athletic and academic development.

Strategic Planning: Balancing Service Commitments and Athletic Development with Academic Goals

Successfully balancing academic goals with specialized commitments requires careful strategic planning that begins well before college enrollment. Whether pursuing athletic opportunities or considering military service pathways, students must develop comprehensive plans that optimize their potential while maintaining strong academic performance.

For students considering military education benefits, understanding and planning for service commitments requires thorough research and preparation. Active duty service members often face unique challenges in coordinating military responsibilities with academic pursuits, frequently necessitating enrollment in online courses or evening classes that accommodate their service schedules. Reservists must carefully plan their academic calendars around monthly drill requirements and potential deployment periods. Creating a detailed education plan that accounts for these military obligations while maximizing available benefits requires careful coordination with military education counselors and academic advisors.

For student-athletes, the planning process requires maintaining peak performance both academically and athletically. Most collegiate athletes dedicate 20-30 hours weekly to their sport through practices, games, travel, and conditioning sessions. This significant time commitment requires exceptional organization and discipline to maintain academic standards. Successful student-athletes typically work closely with academic advisors to select course schedules that accommodate athletic commitments while staying on track for graduation.

Athletic scholarships can come from multiple sources, including NCAA Division I and II programs, as well as NAIA institutions. NAIA schools often provide excellent opportunities for student-athletes who may not meet NCAA Division I requirements or prefer a smaller college environment. Many NAIA institutions offer combination packages of athletic and academic scholarships, making them an attractive option for students who excel in both sports and academics.

Financial planning extends beyond the primary benefits offered by these pathways. Military service members should clearly understand which expenses their benefits cover and which require additional funding sources. Creating comprehensive financial plans that account for both covered and uncovered expenses helps ensure educational goals remain achievable. Similarly, student-athletes need to recognize that most athletic scholarships require annual renewal based on performance standards and aren't guaranteed for four years.

Time management becomes a critical skill for success in either pathway. Military students often benefit from selecting schools with military-friendly policies regarding withdrawals and readmission, protecting their academic progress during periods of active service. Student-athletes learn to maximize every available hour, developing strict study schedules and utilizing academic support services effectively. Many athletic departments provide structured academic support, including tutoring and study halls, which successful student-athletes learn to leverage.

The transition between military service and academic life requires additional planning and support. Many service members benefit from connecting with campus veteran services and other veteran students who understand the unique challenges of this transition. Support services often include assistance with benefit certification, academic advising tailored to military students, and peer mentoring programs that help navigate the shift to civilian student life.

Building a strong support network becomes essential for long-term success. This network might include academic advisors, military education counselors, veteran service officers, coaches, tutors, and peers who understand the unique challenges of balancing specialized commitments with academic goals. Regular check-ins with these support resources help identify and address potential challenges before they impact academic progress.

Successful student-athletes and military service members often develop detailed semester plans that account for all their commitments. These plans typically include daily schedules that allocate specific times for academic work, athletic training, or military duties, as well as essential rest periods. The most successful students learn to be flexible with these schedules while maintaining their core commitments and academic goals.

By approaching these opportunities with thorough planning and disciplined execution, students can successfully balance their service or athletic commitments with their academic goals. The key lies in understanding the full scope of commitments, developing realistic timelines, and maintaining the flexibility to adjust strategies as circumstances change. Through careful planning and utilization of available support services, students can maximize these special funding pathways while achieving their educational objectives. As we conclude our exploration of special funding pathways, it's important to recognize the unique opportunities and responsibilities that come with both military education benefits and athletic scholarships. Military education benefits, including the GI Bill, ROTC programs, and service academies, provide comprehensive funding options while developing valuable leadership skills and career opportunities. These programs require careful consideration of service commitments and long-term obligations, but can offer a clear path to affordable higher education.

Athletic scholarships present opportunities across multiple levels of competition, from NCAA Division I to NAIA programs. While less than 2% of high school athletes receive full Division I scholarships, expanded opportunities through Division II, III, and NAIA institutions provide multiple pathways for student-athletes to fund their education. Success in athletic scholarship pursuits requires exceptional talent, dedication, and realistic expectations about both athletic and academic commitments.

Whether pursuing military benefits or athletic scholarships, the key to success lies in early preparation, thorough research, and maintaining academic excellence throughout the journey. For military pathways, understanding service obligations and program requirements is crucial. ROTC candidates should begin preparing by sophomore year, while service academy applicants need to start even earlier. Athletes must focus on both athletic development and academic achievement, maintaining eligibility standards while navigating the complex recruitment process.

NAIA athletic scholarships deserve special consideration, as they often provide excellent opportunities with more flexibility than NCAA Division I programs. These institutions frequently combine athletic and academic scholarships, creating attractive packages for student-athletes who excel both on the field and in the classroom. The NAIA pathway can be particularly valuable for students seeking a balance between competitive athletics and academic achievement.

Take time to discuss these opportunities with your family, carefully weighing both the benefits and obligations they entail. Consider consulting with military education officers, coaches, and academic advisors who can provide detailed guidance specific to your situation. Remember that these pathways, while potentially rewarding, represent serious commitments that require careful consideration of both immediate advantages and long-term implications.

By approaching these special funding opportunities with informed decision-making and dedicated effort, you can determine if they align with your educational and career goals while potentially providing significant financial support for your college journey. The success stories we've explored demonstrate how these pathways can open doors to affordable higher education while building valuable skills and experience for your future.

Chapter 8:

Understanding Student Loans: Making Informed Borrowing Decisions

Student loans can be either a bridge to educational opportunity or a burden that follows you for decades; the difference often lies in the borrowing decisions you make before signing the first promissory note. As both a parent who helped my children navigate student loans and a counselor who has guided hundreds of families through the borrowing process, I've learned that understanding the full implications of each loan option is crucial for making choices that support rather than hinder your future financial health. Understanding student loans is a critical life skill that can impact your financial well-being for decades after graduation. As you navigate the complex landscape of education financing, it's essential to approach borrowing decisions with careful consideration and a clear understanding of their long-term implications. Just as you wouldn't sign a mortgage without understanding the terms, you shouldn't commit to student loans without fully comprehending their impact on your future.

Early in my counseling career, I worked with a family who taught me a valuable lesson about student loan decisions. The Reeves family came to me after their older daughter had accumulated $98,000 in student loans through a combination of federal and high-interest private loans for her undergraduate degree. Now facing their younger daughter's college decisions, they were determined to make more informed choices. We spent several sessions analyzing different scenarios, calculating monthly payments under various repayment plans, and understanding how interest would accumulate over time. For their younger daughter, we created a strategic borrowing plan that included maximizing federal direct loans before considering any private options, limiting total borrowing to no more than her expected first-year salary in her chosen field, and understanding all repayment options before signing. By making these informed decisions early, their younger daughter graduated with $27,000 in federal loans, a manageable amount given her career path and salary potential. The contrast between the sisters' situations became a powerful example I now share with other families about how understanding loan terms and making strategic borrowing decisions can dramatically impact long-term financial health.

This chapter will guide you through the essential aspects of student loans, from understanding the difference between federal and private options to developing strategies for minimizing your total borrowed amount. We'll explore how to evaluate loan terms, calculate real monthly payment scenarios, and make informed decisions that align with your educational goals and future career prospects. Most importantly, we'll discuss how to avoid common pitfalls that can lead to overwhelming debt and provide practical tools for managing loan responsibilities effectively.

By the end of this chapter, you'll understand the crucial differences between various loan types, know how to calculate the true cost of borrowing over time, and have strategies for minimizing your reliance on loans while maximizing their strategic use when necessary. Remember, student loans can be a valuable tool for accessing education, but like any financial tool, their benefit or burden depends entirely on how wisely they are used.

Federal vs. Private Loans: Understanding Terms, Interest Rates, and Borrower Protections

When it comes to financing your education, understanding the fundamental differences between federal and private student loans can save you thousands of dollars and provide crucial protections for your financial future. Federal student loans, issued by the U.S. Department of Education, offer significant advantages that make them the clear first choice for most students. These loans feature fixed interest rates set annually by Congress; currently ranging from 5.50% to 8.05% for loans disbursed before July 1, 2024, and 6.53% to 9.08% after that date.[70] This predictability in interest rates provides important stability for long-term financial planning.

In contrast, private student loans from banks, credit unions, and other financial institutions can have either fixed or variable rates, typically ranging from 4.19% to 16.69% for fixed rates, with variable rates potentially exceeding 18%.[69, 70, 71] While some private loans might advertise lower initial rates, these often require excellent credit scores and reliable co-signers, and variable rates can increase significantly over time.

One of the most significant advantages of federal loans is their accessibility. Unlike private loans, most federal undergraduate loans don't require a credit check, making them available to students regardless of their credit history or income level.[71, 72] Additionally, federal loans offer unique benefits for students with demonstrated financial need through subsidized loans, where the government pays the interest while you're in school at least half-time. Private loans never offer this valuable subsidy; interest begins accruing immediately upon disbursement.[71]

The repayment terms and borrower protections of federal loans provide crucial safety nets that private loans typically don't match. Federal loans offer multiple repayment plans, including income-driven options that can adjust your monthly payments based on your income and family size. You can also access deferment and forbearance options during periods of economic hardship or further education. Perhaps most importantly, federal loans provide pathways to forgiveness through programs like Public Service Loan Forgiveness and Teacher Loan Forgiveness.[71, 72]

Private loans, while potentially useful for filling funding gaps, come with significantly fewer protections. Repayment terms vary widely between lenders, and many require payments while you're still in school. Most private lenders offer limited, if any, options for modifying repayment terms during financial hardship. There are typically no forgiveness programs available, and discharge options in cases of death or disability are not guaranteed.[71, 72]

When should you consider private loans? Only after you've exhausted all federal loan options. If you need to borrow above federal loan limits and have excellent credit (or a co-signer who does), private loans might be worth exploring.[70, 72] However, it's crucial to carefully compare terms between lenders and understand that you'll be giving up valuable federal protections.

To illustrate the impact of these differences, consider a student borrowing $30,000 for their education. With a federal loan at a fixed 6.53% interest rate on a standard 10-year repayment plan, their monthly payment would be approximately $342. The same amount borrowed through a private lender at 12% interest would result in monthly payments of roughly $430, a difference of $88 per month, or over $10,500 over the life of the loan. Moreover, if the federal loan borrower faces financial hardship, they can switch to an income-driven repayment plan, potentially lowering their monthly payment significantly. The private loan borrower would have few, if any, options for payment relief.

Before accepting any student loan, carefully review all terms and conditions. For federal loans, complete the FAFSA as early as possible to ensure access to the full range of federal aid options. If you must consider private loans, compare offers from multiple lenders, paying close attention to interest rates, repayment terms, and any fees. Remember that the lowest advertised rate may not be the rate you qualify for, and variable rates can increase significantly over time.

Loan Repayment Strategies: Income-Driven Plans, Forgiveness Programs, and Early Payoff Options

Understanding and selecting the right repayment strategy for your student loans can significantly impact your long-term financial health. With various options available through federal loan programs, borrowers can tailor their repayment approach to match their financial circumstances and career paths. Let's explore the key repayment strategies that can help make your student loan debt more manageable.

Income-driven repayment (IDR) plans offer a lifeline for borrowers whose loan payments would otherwise be unmanageable relative to their income.[58] These plans calculate your monthly payment based on a percentage of your discretionary income, typically extending the repayment period to 20-25 years. For example, if you have $50,000 in federal student loans and earn $40,000 annually, your payment under an IDR plan might be around $180 per month, compared to $530 under the standard 10-year repayment plan. However, it's important to note that while IDR plans lower monthly payments, they often result in paying more interest over time.

Public Service Loan Forgiveness (PSLF) represents one of the most significant opportunities for debt relief, particularly for those committed to public service careers. After making 120 qualifying monthly payments while working full-time for an eligible employer, the remaining balance is forgiven tax-free. Teachers working in low-income schools may qualify for up to $17,500 in forgiveness after five consecutive years of service through the Teacher Loan Forgiveness program. These programs require careful attention to eligibility requirements and documentation to ensure you stay on track for forgiveness.

For borrowers able to make more than the minimum payments, early payoff strategies can significantly reduce the total interest paid over the life of the loans. The debt avalanche method, which focuses extra payments on the highest-interest loans first, provides the greatest mathematical benefit. For instance, if you have multiple loans ranging from 4% to 8% interest, directing any extra payments to the 8% loan first will save the most money in interest charges. Alternatively, the debt snowball method targets the smallest balances first, providing psychological wins that can help maintain motivation for debt repayment.

Bi-weekly payments represent another effective strategy for accelerating loan repayment. Instead of making one monthly payment, splitting it into two bi-weekly payments results in 26 half-payments annually, equivalent to 13 monthly payments instead of 12. This simple change can reduce a 10-year repayment period by several months and save thousands in interest charges.

However, it's crucial to remember that the best strategy for managing student loan debt is minimizing borrowing from the start.[17, 5, 95] Consider alternatives like community college transfer pathways, in-state public universities, and merit scholarships before taking on significant loan debt. Many employers also offer tuition assistance programs that can help reduce the need for borrowing.

When evaluating repayment options, consider your long-term financial goals. Student loan debt can impact major life decisions like homeownership, retirement savings, and career choices.[58] The current student loan crisis has demonstrated how educational debt can contribute to delayed financial milestones and reduced economic participation. Therefore, choosing the right repayment strategy isn't just about managing monthly payments; it's about creating a foundation for long-term financial success.

Regardless of which repayment strategy you choose, stay informed about your loans and review your repayment plan annually. Income-driven plans require annual recertification, and your financial circumstances may change, making a different repayment strategy more appropriate. Keep detailed records of all payments and communications with loan servicers, especially if you're pursuing loan forgiveness programs.

Parent PLUS Loans: Weighing the Pros and Cons of Parent Borrowing

Parent PLUS loans represent a significant decision point for many families in the college financing journey, offering both opportunities and potential pitfalls that require careful consideration. These federal loans allow parents to borrow up to the full cost of attendance minus any other financial aid received,[74] providing a seemingly straightforward solution to funding gaps. However, this unlimited borrowing capacity, while beneficial in the short term, can create substantial long-term financial challenges for families if not approached strategically.

The fundamental features of Parent PLUS loans include standardized interest rates that don't vary based on credit scores, though they typically carry higher rates than direct student loans.[74] For example, while undergraduate federal loans currently have interest rates around 5.50%, Parent PLUS loans often carry rates several percentage points higher. Additionally, these loans include origination fees that further increase the cost of borrowing.[75] Understanding these costs is crucial; on a $20,000 loan, the origination fee alone could add hundreds of dollars to the amount owed before any interest accrues.

One of the most significant advantages of Parent PLUS loans is their accessibility and federal backing. Parents who pass a basic credit check can secure funding regardless of their income level or credit score,[74] providing a reliable option when other financing sources fall short. The loans also come with certain federal protections[76] and flexible repayment options, including extended and graduated repayment plans that can stretch payments over periods ranging from 10 to 25 years.[73]

However, the drawbacks of Parent PLUS loans warrant serious consideration. Unlike student loans, there's no automatic grace period; repayment begins immediately after disbursement unless parents specifically request deferment while their student is enrolled at least half-time.[77] Interest continues to accrue during deferment periods, potentially adding thousands to the loan balance before repayment begins. Additionally, Parent PLUS loans have limited access to income-driven repayment options, with only Income-Contingent Repayment (ICR) available, and only after consolidation.[77]

The timing of Parent PLUS loans can also create significant challenges for family financial planning. Parents who take these loans in their 50s could still be making payments well into their retirement years if they opt for extended repayment plans.[77] This extended timeline can seriously impact retirement security and other long-term financial goals. For instance, a parent borrowing $50,000 in PLUS loans at age 50 could still be making payments at age 75 under a 25-year repayment plan.

Before committing to Parent PLUS loans, families should explore all other financing options. This includes maximizing federal student loans, which typically offer better terms,[74] pursuing scholarships and grants, and considering cost-effective alternatives like community college transfer programs. Some families find success with a shared approach, where students take responsibility for federal student loans up to their limits, while parents consider a more modest PLUS loan amount to fill any remaining gaps.

If Parent PLUS loans become necessary, establish clear borrowing limits based on realistic repayment capabilities. Consider the monthly payment impact - a $30,000 PLUS loan under standard repayment could require monthly payments of around $350, depending on current interest rates. Multiply this by four years of borrowing, and the monthly obligation becomes substantial.

The tax implications of Parent PLUS loans offer some relief through potential interest deductions of up to $2,500 annually, depending on income levels.[73] However, these benefits shouldn't be the primary factor in borrowing decisions, as they only marginally offset the total cost of borrowing.

Ultimately, the decision to take Parent PLUS loans should align with both the family's immediate education funding needs and long-term financial security.[74, 77] While these loans can bridge important funding gaps, they should be approached with careful consideration of their impact on retirement planning, other financial obligations, and the family's overall financial health. Remember, the ability to borrow doesn't always align with the wisdom of doing so, especially when it comes to education financing that could affect family finances for decades to come. As we conclude our exploration of student loans and borrowing decisions, it's crucial to remember that student loans, while often necessary, should be approached as part of a comprehensive college funding strategy rather than the primary solution. Throughout this chapter, we've examined how informed borrowing decisions can dramatically impact your financial future, from understanding the critical differences between federal and private loans to exploring repayment strategies that align with your career goals.

The contrast between the Reeves sisters' experiences, one graduating with $98,000 in mixed loans and the other with $27,000 in manageable federal loans, illustrates how knowledge and strategic planning can significantly impact long-term financial outcomes. Their story reminds us that it's not just about accessing loans, but about making informed choices that support rather than hinder your future financial health.

Key takeaways from this chapter include the importance of exhausting federal loan options before considering private loans, understanding the true cost of borrowing through careful calculation of interest rates and repayment terms, and recognizing how different repayment strategies can affect your long-term financial stability. We've also explored how Parent PLUS loans, while providing important funding options, require careful consideration of their impact on family financial security and retirement planning.

As you move forward with your college funding decisions, remember that student loans are just one piece of the larger college financing puzzle. The most successful approaches typically combine multiple strategies, from maximizing grants and scholarships to leveraging work-study opportunities and choosing cost-effective education paths. By understanding your loan options and their implications before signing any promissory notes, you can make borrowing decisions that support your educational goals while protecting your financial future.

Perhaps most importantly, this chapter emphasizes that there's no one-size-fits-all approach to student loans. Your borrowing strategy should align with your specific circumstances, career goals, and family financial situation. Whether you're considering federal loans, evaluating Parent PLUS options, or exploring private lending, the key is to make informed decisions based on a clear understanding of terms, conditions, and long-term implications.

As a final reminder, always view student loans as a tool to be used strategically rather than as a default solution for college funding. By combining the knowledge gained from this chapter with the other strategies discussed throughout this book, you can create a college financing plan that minimizes debt while maximizing educational opportunities. Your future self will thank you for the time invested in understanding and carefully planning your approach to student loans today.

Chapter 9:

Work-Study and Part-Time Employment: Earning While Learning

One of the most overlooked strategies for reducing college costs is the strategic combination of work and study opportunities available to students during their college years. Beyond just earning money, these opportunities can provide valuable work experience, professional connections, and in some cases, even direct connections to future career paths. The strategic combination of employment and academics not only helps offset college costs but can provide invaluable real-world experience that enhances both your education and future career prospects. As your guide through this crucial aspect of college planning, I've seen firsthand how students who carefully balance work and studies often develop superior time management skills and graduate with less debt than their peers.

One particularly powerful opportunity that many students overlook is cooperative education (co-op) programs, especially in STEM fields. These structured programs allow students to alternate between full-time study and full-time paid work experiences throughout their college career. Unlike traditional part-time jobs, co-op positions typically offer competitive salaries and direct experience in your field of study. For example, engineering students might spend one quarter taking classes, followed by a quarter working at a major technology company, continuing this pattern throughout their degree program. These positions not only provide substantial income to offset college costs but often lead to full-time job offers upon graduation.

During my years as a high school counselor, I worked with a student named Jamie who was concerned about affording college despite receiving partial financial aid. Together, we explored work-study opportunities at her chosen university and discovered that the campus library offered positions specifically for work-study students that aligned perfectly with her class schedule. Jamie applied early and secured a position that allowed her to work 12 hours per week during the semester. The library position not only provided steady income but also offered quiet periods during evening shifts when she could study while staffing the desk. By her sophomore year, Jamie had been promoted to a student supervisor role with a higher hourly rate, and she discovered that her work experience helped her develop valuable time management skills. She maintained a 3.7 GPA while earning approximately $3,500 per academic year through work-study, significantly reducing her need for additional student loans. Jamie's success story demonstrates how strategic selection of work opportunities can support both financial and academic goals while building valuable professional skills.

In this chapter, we'll explore the various ways students can effectively combine employment with their academic pursuits. We'll examine federal work-study programs, which provide eligible students with part-time jobs that often align with their course schedules and career interests. You'll learn how to identify and secure campus employment opportunities that offer flexibility and valuable experience. Most importantly, we'll discuss strategies for maintaining academic excellence while working, ensuring that employment enhances rather than hinders your college experience.

Whether you're considering federal work-study positions, on-campus jobs, co-op programs, or off-campus employment, understanding how to navigate these opportunities can significantly impact your college financing strategy. We'll explore how to evaluate different employment options, manage your time effectively, and make the most of both the financial and professional development benefits that come with working while in school. The goal is to help you create a balanced approach that supports both your academic success and financial well-being.

Federal Work-Study Programs: Understanding Eligibility, Benefits, and Application Process

Federal Work-Study (FWS) represents one of the most valuable yet often underutilized components of federal financial aid. This program provides eligible students with part-time employment opportunities that can significantly reduce college costs while building valuable work experience. Understanding how to maximize these opportunities requires knowledge of both the basic requirements and strategic approaches to securing the most beneficial positions.

To qualify for Federal Work-Study, students must first demonstrate financial need through the FAFSA application process. Eligibility requirements include enrollment at least half-time in an eligible degree program at a participating institution, maintaining satisfactory academic progress, and having either U.S. citizenship or eligible non-citizen status. It's important to note that not all colleges and universities participate in the FWS program, so checking with your institution's financial aid office is an essential first step.

The benefits of Federal Work-Study extend far beyond the paycheck. While students earn at least the federal minimum wage (often more, depending on the position and location), the program offers several unique advantages over traditional part-time employment. FWS positions typically provide flexible scheduling that accommodates class times, with most students working 10-20 hours per week during the academic year. Unlike student loans, these earnings don't need to be repaid, making FWS an attractive option for reducing overall college debt.

One particularly valuable aspect of FWS is that many positions align with students' academic and career interests. For example, education majors might work as tutors, while business students could gain experience in campus offices. These positions often provide networking opportunities with faculty and staff, potentially leading to strong references or future job opportunities. Additionally, FWS earnings are typically exempt from the expected family contribution calculation on the following year's FAFSA, making it a more advantageous form of student income.

The application process begins with completing the FAFSA, where students should indicate their interest in work-study opportunities. If eligible, the work-study award will appear as part of the financial aid package. However, receiving an award doesn't guarantee employment; students must still actively search for and secure positions through their institution's job placement system. Many schools offer a variety of roles, from library assistants and research aides to administrative support positions.

The financial impact of FWS can be substantial. Students working 15 hours per week at the federal minimum wage can earn approximately $4,350 over two semesters. However, many positions pay more than minimum wage, and some students find opportunities to earn up to their full award amount, which could exceed $5,000 annually, depending on their financial aid package. These earnings can significantly reduce the need for additional student loans or family contributions.

To maximize FWS benefits, students should apply for the FAFSA as early as possible, ideally right when it opens on October 1st for the following academic year. This early application increases the chances of receiving a work-study award, as funds are limited and distributed on a first-come, first-served basis. Additionally, once awarded, students should begin their job search early, as desirable positions often fill quickly at the start of each semester.

It's crucial to understand that FWS earnings are capped at the total amount awarded in the financial aid package. Students and supervisors must carefully monitor hours worked to ensure they don't exceed their award amount. Some institutions offer the flexibility to increase awards if additional funds become available, but this isn't guaranteed and should be discussed with the financial aid office.

The program also includes opportunities for community service work, with many institutions required to use at least 7% of their FWS allocation for community service positions. These roles often involve working with local non-profit organizations or public agencies, providing valuable experience while serving the community. Such positions can be particularly beneficial for students interested in public service careers or those seeking to build a strong résumé with meaningful volunteer experience.

Campus Employment: Finding and Securing On-Campus Jobs Beyond Work-Study

Beyond Federal Work-Study positions, colleges and universities offer numerous employment opportunities that provide students with valuable work experience and steady income. These positions, available to all students regardless of financial aid status, can significantly contribute to college affordability while building professional skills and networks that benefit future careers.

A particularly valuable option that many students overlook is participation in cooperative education (co-op) programs, especially prevalent in STEM fields. These structured programs allow students to alternate between full-time study and paid work experiences throughout their college career. For example, a student might attend classes for one quarter or semester, then work full-time at a partner company the next period, continuing this pattern throughout their degree program. Co-op positions typically offer competitive salaries and direct experience in your field of study, with engineering and technology students often earning $15-25 per hour or more. These programs not only help offset college costs but frequently lead to full-time job offers upon graduation.

Traditional on-campus jobs typically offer several distinct advantages over off-campus employment. Most notably, these positions provide unmatched convenience and flexibility, with work locations just minutes from classes and schedules designed to accommodate academic commitments. Students generally work 15-20 hours per week, allowing them to maintain focus on their studies while earning a meaningful income. For example, at many institutions, student workers earn well above minimum wage, with some positions paying $15-20 per hour in 2024, making these positions an attractive option for reducing college expenses.

To find and secure on-campus employment, students should begin their search early and utilize multiple channels. The first stop should be the institution's online job board or career portal, where new positions are regularly posted. These platforms typically list openings across various departments, from library assistant roles to research positions within academic departments. Additionally, visiting the Office of Student Employment can provide valuable insights into available opportunities and application procedures.

When applying for campus positions, students should prepare professional application materials, including a tailored resume and cover letter that highlight relevant skills and experiences. Many roles require basic professional skills such as communication, organization, and reliability. Students should emphasize these qualities in their applications, even if they don't have extensive work experience.

Popular on-campus positions include library assistants, research assistants, tutors, campus tour guides, and office assistants. Each role offers unique benefits beyond the paycheck. For instance, library assistants often have quiet periods during their shifts when they can study, while research assistants gain valuable experience in their field of study. Tour guides develop public speaking skills and deep knowledge of campus resources, while office assistants learn professional workplace protocols and administrative skills.

The networking opportunities provided by campus employment shouldn't be underestimated. Working within academic departments or administrative offices allows students to build relationships with faculty, staff, and peers who can later serve as professional references or mentors. These connections often prove invaluable when seeking internships or full-time employment after graduation.

To maximize the benefits of campus employment, students should approach their job search strategically. This includes:

- Checking job boards frequently, as new positions often become available throughout the semester
- Visiting specific departments of interest to inquire about potential openings
- Utilizing career center resources for resume review and interview preparation
- Maintaining professional communication throughout the application process
- Being prepared to start work early in the semester when many positions open

While wages vary by institution and position, campus employment can significantly reduce the need for additional student loans. For example, a student working 15 hours per week at $15 per hour could earn approximately $3,600 per semester before taxes. This income can help cover essential expenses like textbooks, supplies, and personal needs without increasing loan debt.

It's important to note that international students may also be eligible for on-campus employment, though they typically face certain hour restrictions. These students should consult with their institution's international student office to understand specific guidelines and limitations before seeking employment.

Successful campus employment requires balancing work responsibilities with academic commitments. Most institutions design their student employment programs to support academic success, recognizing that students are scholars first and employees second. This philosophy creates a supportive work environment where supervisors understand and accommodate academic priorities, making campus employment an ideal option for students seeking to gain work experience while managing their studies effectively.

Strategic Job Selection: Balancing Income Potential with Academic Success

Selecting the right job during college requires careful consideration of both earning potential and academic impact. While the allure of higher-paying positions might be strong, the primary goal must remain academic success. Research shows that students who work 10-15 hours per week often perform better academically than those who don't work at all, but performance typically begins to decline when work hours exceed 20 hours per week consistently.

Cooperative education (co-op) programs offer an excellent opportunity to maximize both income and career development, particularly in STEM fields. These structured programs alternate academic quarters or semesters with full-time paid work experience at partner companies. For example, an engineering student might spend the fall semester in classes, then work full-time during the spring semester at a technology company, earning significant income while gaining invaluable industry experience. Many co-op positions pay competitive salaries, ranging from $18-35 per hour, allowing students to earn substantial income during their work terms while maintaining full focus on academics during study terms.

When evaluating traditional employment opportunities, students should prioritize positions that offer maximum earnings with minimum time investment. High-paying service industry jobs, such as restaurant serving positions at upscale establishments or customer service roles with evening and weekend hours, can provide significant income while accommodating class schedules. Additionally, career-relevant paid internships offer dual benefits of competitive wages and professional development, potentially leading to full-time employment after graduation.

On-campus employment, particularly through Federal Work-Study programs, offers unique advantages that support academic success. These positions typically feature convenient locations, supervisors who understand academic priorities, and flexible scheduling around class times. Departmental positions within your field of study can provide valuable networking opportunities with faculty while often allowing study time during slower periods.

To maximize income potential while protecting academic performance, consider implementing these key strategies:

- Target higher-wage positions with opportunities for tips or commission
- Concentrate work hours during academic breaks and summer months
- Create buffer periods before major exams or projects
- Combine steady part-time work with flexible gig opportunities

Time management becomes crucial when balancing work and academics. Successful students often employ block scheduling with dedicated study periods, use digital calendar systems to track deadlines and work shifts, and develop study efficiency methods to maximize productive hours. Communication with employers about academic priorities is essential, particularly during exam periods.

Technology has created new opportunities for students to earn income with unprecedented flexibility. Remote work positions, online tutoring platforms, and gig economy services allow students to earn money while maintaining control over their schedules. These technology-enabled options can provide significant income while accommodating the varying demands of academic life.

When selecting a job, carefully evaluate the employer's flexibility regarding exam schedules, ability to adjust shifts on short notice, and seasonal accommodation of academic demands. Consider location efficiency to minimize commute time and transportation costs. Additionally, look for positions with growth potential, including opportunities for wage increases and skill development relevant to your career goals.

One effective approach, particularly for students pursuing a debt-free degree, involves starting at a community college while living at home. This strategy allows students to maintain a consistent work schedule while minimizing expenses during the initial college years. Students can build savings before transferring to a university, potentially qualifying for transfer scholarships in the process.

Remember that while earning potential is important, preserving academic performance must remain the priority. The ideal job provides not just income, but also supports your educational goals through flexible scheduling, understanding supervision, and opportunities for professional growth. By carefully selecting employment that aligns with both financial needs and academic requirements, students can successfully navigate the challenges of working while pursuing their degree. As we conclude our exploration of work opportunities during college, it's essential to recognize that earning while learning represents more than just a way to offset college costs; it's an investment in both your education and your future career. Throughout this chapter, we've explored how strategic employment choices, from Federal Work-Study positions to co-op programs and campus jobs, can significantly impact your college financing strategy while building valuable professional skills.

The power of co-operative education programs, particularly in STEM fields, stands out as a transformative opportunity. By alternating between academic terms and full-time paid work experiences, students can earn substantial income while gaining invaluable industry experience. These structured programs offer competitive salaries and often lead to full-time employment opportunities after graduation, making them an excellent option for students seeking to minimize debt while maximizing career preparation.

Jamie's story, which opened our discussion of campus employment, perfectly illustrates how thoughtful job selection and careful time management can lead to both financial and professional success. Her library position not only provided steady income but also created an environment conducive to maintaining strong academic performance. Like Jamie, many students discover that the right employment opportunity can provide much more than a paycheck; it can offer professional connections, skill development, and real-world experience that complement classroom learning.

As you consider your own path to combining work and study, remember these key takeaways:

- Begin your job search early, particularly for Federal Work-Study positions, where funds are limited
- Consider co-op programs that combine paid work experience with academic studies
- Prioritize positions that offer flexibility around academic schedules
- Look for opportunities that align with your career interests and academic goals
- Consider the total value proposition of each job, including location, networking potential, and skill development
- Maintain clear communication with employers about academic priorities

The decision to work during college should be approached thoughtfully, with careful consideration of your academic capabilities, time management skills, and financial needs. While the additional income can significantly reduce your reliance on student loans, the experience gained through meaningful employment often proves just as valuable as the earnings themselves.

Most importantly, remember that success in combining work and academics requires regular evaluation and adjustment of your approach. What works in your freshman year may need modification as course loads increase or academic demands change. Stay flexible, maintain open communication with both employers and academic advisors, and never hesitate to adjust your work schedule to protect your academic success.

As both a parent and counselor, I've witnessed countless students successfully navigate the challenges of working while pursuing their degree. Their experiences consistently show that with proper planning, strategic job selection, and strong time management skills, employment during college can become a valuable component of both your educational funding strategy and your professional development journey.

As you move forward in your college planning, use the strategies and insights from this chapter to create your own pathway to successful employment during your college years. Whether through Federal Work-Study, campus employment, co-op programs, or off-campus opportunities, remember that the right job can do more than just help pay for college; it can enhance your entire educational experience and prepare you for future career success.

Chapter 10:

Advanced Cost-Cutting Strategies: Negotiation, Tax Benefits, and Hidden Savings

While many families accept their initial financial aid offers as final, understanding advanced cost-cutting strategies can unlock thousands in additional savings through strategic negotiation and smart financial planning. The difference between paying full price and securing significant discounts often lies in knowing how to effectively advocate for better aid packages, maximize tax benefits, and identify hidden savings opportunities that most families overlook. For many families, the difference between manageable college costs and overwhelming debt often lies in understanding and implementing advanced cost-reduction strategies that go beyond basic financial aid applications. These sophisticated approaches, from negotiating aid packages to maximizing tax benefits, can unlock substantial savings that many families leave unclaimed simply because they don't know these opportunities exist.

I've witnessed countless families transform their college funding outlook by mastering these advanced strategies. Take the Chen family's journey, which perfectly illustrates the power of combining multiple cost-cutting approaches. When they first came to my office, they were discouraged by the initial financial aid package offered to their daughter, Lisa. Instead of accepting what seemed like a final offer, we developed a comprehensive strategy that would ultimately save them over $100,000 across four years.

We began by preparing a strategic financial aid appeal, carefully documenting their special circumstances, including recent medical expenses and a younger sibling's upcoming college enrollment. After researching comparable aid packages from competing institutions, the family crafted a professional appeal letter that demonstrated both their genuine need and their strong commitment to the university. Through persistent but respectful negotiation with the financial aid office, they secured an additional $8,500 in annual grant aid and a $3,000 yearly merit scholarship.

But the Chen family's success didn't stop with financial aid negotiation. By coordinating their 529 plan withdrawals with the American Opportunity Tax Credit, they maximized their tax benefits, saving an additional $2,500 each year. They also discovered creative cost-cutting opportunities, including having Lisa serve as a Resident Advisor during her sophomore year, which saved $12,000 in housing costs.

Their story exemplifies how combining negotiation skills, tax planning, and creative cost-reduction strategies can dramatically impact the overall cost of college education. More importantly, it demonstrates that families who arm themselves with knowledge about these advanced strategies can actively shape their financial outcomes rather than passively accepting initial offers.

In this chapter, we'll explore these sophisticated cost-cutting approaches in detail, providing you with the tools and knowledge to implement similar strategies in your own college funding journey. From understanding the nuances of financial aid appeals to maximizing education-related tax benefits, you'll learn how to identify and capitalize on opportunities that many families miss. Remember, in the complex landscape of college funding, sometimes the most significant savings come from knowing not just what to ask for, but how to ask for it effectively.

Financial Aid Appeal Strategies: Negotiating Better Aid Packages and Merit Awards

One of the most powerful yet underutilized strategies for reducing college costs is the financial aid appeal process. While many families accept their initial aid package as final, understanding how to effectively appeal these offers can potentially unlock thousands of dollars in additional funding. The appeal process, officially known as a "professional judgment review" or "special circumstances review," exists because standardized financial aid formulas cannot account for every family's unique situation.[88]

Successful appeals typically fall into two main categories: those based on financial circumstances and those leveraging merit or competitive offers. Financial circumstances that warrant appeals include job loss, medical expenses not covered by insurance, support of extended family members, or natural disasters affecting family finances.[88] Merit-based appeals often stem from improved academic performance or stronger competitive offers from similar institutions.

The key to a successful appeal lies in proper documentation and timing. Before initiating an appeal, gather all relevant documentation that substantiates your case.[91] This might include medical bills, layoff notices, bank statements showing financial changes, or competing financial aid award letters from other institutions.[90] Timing is crucial, while appeals can be made at any point when circumstances change,[90] submitting your appeal early in the process often provides access to more uncommitted aid funds.[91]

When crafting your appeal letter, maintain a formal and respectful tone while being specific about dates and dollar amounts. The letter should be concise (1-2 pages) and focus on circumstances beyond your control.[88, 90] Begin with a clear statement of purpose, followed by a detailed explanation of your special circumstances, preferably organized with the most significant financial impacts listed first.[88]

The appeal process follows a specific structure that requires careful attention to detail. First, contact the college's financial aid office to understand their specific appeal procedures, required forms, and documentation requirements.[88, 89] Some institutions have formal appeal forms, while others may request a detailed letter. Submit all materials according to the institution's preferred method, whether through an online portal, email, or mail.[90]

After submission, follow up approximately one week later to confirm receipt of your appeal materials. Be prepared to respond promptly to any requests for additional information.[90] While the review process typically takes 1-4 weeks, this can vary by institution and proximity to enrollment deadlines.[91] Maintain professional persistence in seeking a decision while remaining patient with the process.

When appealing based on competing offers, provide copies of other financial aid award letters from similar institutions. This approach can be particularly effective when the competing institutions are of similar academic caliber. Focus on demonstrating your strong fit with the institution's values and goals while emphasizing your commitment to attend if financial barriers can be reduced.

Remember that financial aid offices want to help students attend their institutions, but they need to see legitimate need backed by evidence.[88] A well-documented appeal that clearly demonstrates significant changes in financial circumstances or compelling competitive offers can result in thousands of additional dollars in aid. The difference between a successful and unsuccessful appeal often lies in the quality of documentation and the professionalism of the approach.

While there's no guarantee that an appeal will result in additional aid, the potential benefits make it worth the effort. Even a modest increase in financial aid can significantly impact your college funding strategy. Approach the process with thorough preparation, clear documentation, and professional persistence, and you may find yourself with a more manageable college financial picture.

Education Tax Benefits: Understanding and Maximizing Credits, Deductions, and Savings Incentives

Understanding and properly utilizing education tax benefits can significantly reduce your overall college costs, yet many families leave thousands of dollars in tax savings unclaimed each year. The U.S. tax code offers several valuable benefits for students and families pursuing higher education, with the American Opportunity Tax Credit

(AOTC) standing out as one of the most substantial opportunities for savings during undergraduate years.

The AOTC provides a tax credit of up to $2,500 per eligible student per year for the first four years of higher education.[92, 95] What makes this credit particularly valuable is its structure; you can claim 100% of the first $2,000 in qualified education expenses, plus 25% of the next $2,000.[94] Even better, if the credit reduces your tax liability to zero, you can receive up to 40% of the remaining credit (maximum $1,000) as a refund.[95] For a family with an eligible student, this means potentially reducing college costs by $10,000 over four years of undergraduate education.

Qualified expenses for the AOTC include tuition, required fees, and course materials needed for attendance and paid during the tax year.[92] However, it's crucial to note that income limitations apply; the credit begins phasing out for individuals earning $80,000 ($160,000 for joint filers).[93] Proper timing and documentation of expenses are essential for maximizing this benefit.

For students who don't qualify for the AOTC or who are beyond their first four years of education, the Lifetime Learning Credit (LLC) offers an alternative opportunity for tax savings. The LLC provides a maximum credit of $2,000 per tax return, calculated as 20% of the first $10,000 spent on qualified tuition and related expenses.[93] Unlike the AOTC, there's no limit on the number of years you can claim this credit,[93] making it particularly valuable for graduate students or those pursuing professional degree programs.

Strategic planning is crucial for maximizing these tax benefits. Consider coordinating the timing of education expenses to optimize credit eligibility across tax years. For example, if you're close to the $4,000 expense limit for the AOTC in one year, you might benefit from postponing additional qualified expenses until January of the following tax year to ensure maximum credit utilization.

Proper documentation is essential for claiming education tax benefits. Keep detailed records of all qualified education expenses, maintain copies of Form 1098-T from eligible educational institutions, and carefully track any scholarships or grants received. These records will be crucial when preparing your tax returns and can help prevent valuable tax savings from being left unclaimed.

Looking ahead, it's important to note that significant changes may be coming to education tax benefits. Current proposals under consideration include potential eliminations of several key benefits, including the AOTC, LLC, and the exclusion of scholarship and fellowship income.[93] These changes could have substantial financial implications for families planning for college expenses.

For working professionals pursuing additional education, don't overlook employer-provided educational assistance programs, which may offer up to $5,250 in tax-free education benefits. Additionally, work-related education that maintains or improves skills required for your current job may qualify for business deductions.

To maximize these benefits, consider working with a tax professional who specializes in education benefits, particularly when coordinating multiple tax advantages. The complexity of education tax benefits means that professional guidance can often help ensure you're not leaving money on the table while maintaining compliance with tax regulations.

Remember that tax benefits represent just one component of a comprehensive college funding strategy. By understanding and properly utilizing these benefits in conjunction with other funding sources, you can significantly reduce the overall cost of higher education while ensuring compliance with tax regulations and maximizing available benefits.

Hidden Cost Reduction Opportunities: Housing, Textbooks, and Campus Life Expenses

Beyond tuition and fees, a significant portion of college costs comes from what many families initially overlook: housing, textbooks, and daily campus life expenses. These "hidden" costs can add thousands to your annual college expenses, but with strategic planning and informed decisions, you can substantially reduce these expenses without sacrificing your educational experience or quality of life.

Textbooks represent one of the most controllable yet significant expenses, with individual books potentially costing up to $400 and average prices ranging between $100 and $150.[98] With textbook prices increasing by approximately 6% annually, this expense can quickly accumulate across multiple courses. However, research shows that 66% of students successfully reduce these costs by purchasing used textbooks, while 48% find free versions online.[96]

To minimize textbook expenses, timing is crucial. Begin your search for course materials as soon as syllabi become available, as the best deals on used textbooks disappear quickly. Explore multiple sources, including campus bookstores, online marketplaces like Amazon and AbeBooks, and digital alternatives.[98] Many institutions now offer inclusive access programs where publishers provide discounted digital versions through direct institutional partnerships.[97] Additionally, an increasing number of professors are adopting Open Educational Resources (OER), which provide quality educational content at no cost to students.[98]

Housing often represents the second-largest expense after tuition, but numerous strategies can help reduce these costs. On campus, consider applying for Resident Assistant (RA) positions, which typically offer free or significantly reduced housing in exchange for supervisory responsibilities. For off-campus options, carefully evaluate the trade-offs between convenience and cost; housing prices often decrease substantially with distance from campus. Living with multiple roommates can dramatically reduce individual costs, while negotiating longer lease terms or early payment arrangements may secure better rates.

Campus life expenses, while individually smaller, can accumulate significantly over an academic year. Meal plan optimization presents a major opportunity for savings; carefully analyze your actual eating habits before committing to an extensive meal plan. Many students find they can reduce costs by combining a smaller meal plan with strategic use of community kitchens for meal preparation. Transportation costs can be minimized by taking advantage of campus shuttle services and student discounts on local transit systems.

Technology and academic materials represent another area where strategic planning can yield substantial savings. Before purchasing expensive equipment or software, investigate campus computer labs and library resources. Many institutions offer free printing, scanning, and software access through campus facilities. Additionally, numerous technology companies provide significant educational discounts on essential software and hardware.

Institutional support programs can provide crucial assistance with hidden costs. Many colleges have established emergency assistance funds, textbook lending libraries, and basic needs initiatives to help students manage unexpected expenses. These programs often go underutilized simply because students don't know they exist. Make it a priority to research and understand all available support programs at your chosen institution.

The impact of these cost-reduction strategies can be substantial. For example, one documented case showed two college freshmen spending just $329.25 total on textbooks over two quarters at different institutions, primarily through strategic use of used books and OER materials.[99] This represents significant savings compared to the potential cost of new textbooks, which could have exceeded $1,500 for the same period.

To maximize your savings on these hidden costs, develop a comprehensive plan before the academic year begins. Research all available options, from housing alternatives to textbook sources, and create a realistic budget that accounts for all expenses. Remember that many of these costs are negotiable or have multiple alternatives; don't accept the first or most obvious option without exploring alternatives.

Most importantly, take advantage of institutional resources and support programs designed to help students manage these expenses effectively. Throughout this chapter, we've explored sophisticated strategies that can dramatically reduce college costs through active negotiation, smart tax planning, and uncovering hidden savings opportunities. The Chen family's success story demonstrates how combining these approaches can lead to substantial reductions in college expenses; in their case, over $100,000 across four years. Their experience shows that the difference between managing college costs effectively and struggling with overwhelming debt often lies in understanding and implementing these advanced strategies.

While navigating financial aid appeals, tax benefits, and hidden costs might seem daunting at first, remember that each of these areas presents opportunities for significant savings. A well-crafted financial aid appeal, supported by proper documentation and professional presentation, can unlock thousands in additional aid. Understanding and properly utilizing education tax benefits like the American Opportunity Tax Credit can provide up to $2,500 annually per eligible student. Meanwhile, strategic approaches to managing textbooks, housing, and campus life expenses can yield substantial savings without compromising educational quality.

As you implement these strategies, remember that timing and documentation are crucial. Start early in researching and understanding your options, maintain detailed records of all expenses and communications, and don't hesitate to seek professional guidance when needed. The investment of time in understanding and implementing these advanced cost-cutting strategies can yield returns far greater than the effort required.

Perhaps most importantly, these strategies demonstrate that families have more control over college costs than they might initially believe. Whether through negotiating better aid packages, maximizing tax benefits, or finding creative ways to reduce expenses, proactive families can significantly impact their college funding outcomes. The key lies in approaching college costs not as fixed amounts but as starting points for negotiation and optimization.

As you move forward in your college funding journey, remember that success often comes from combining multiple strategies rather than relying on a single approach. Like the Chen family, consider how you can layer different cost-reduction methods, from aid appeals to tax benefits to lifestyle choices, to create a comprehensive plan that makes college more affordable. With careful planning, strategic thinking, and persistent effort, you can significantly reduce the financial burden of higher education while maintaining focus on what matters most: achieving your educational goals.

The strategies and approaches we've discussed in this chapter represent some of the most powerful tools available for making college more affordable. By understanding and implementing these advanced cost-cutting methods, you're well-equipped to navigate the financial challenges of higher education while minimizing the impact on your family's financial health. Remember, every dollar saved through these strategies is one less dollar needed in loans or family contributions, so making the effort to master these approaches is well worth your time and energy.

Conclusion

As we conclude our exploration of college financing strategies, the most crucial takeaway is that successfully funding higher education requires a comprehensive approach, combining multiple tools and opportunities that add up to meet the total cost of attendance. Just as the Martinez family demonstrated in our opening chapter, it's about building a strategic plan that leverages every available resource, from early academic planning to financial aid optimization.

Throughout this book, we've examined numerous pathways to make college more affordable, from maximizing dual credit opportunities to understanding the intricacies of financial aid packages. The success stories we've shared, like Sarah earning 36 college credits in high school and Emma securing $22,000 in local scholarships, prove that combining multiple strategies can dramatically reduce the total cost of education. These examples aren't isolated successes but blueprints for your own college funding journey.

Keep this book readily accessible throughout your child's high school years. Reference it as you approach each new phase, from freshman course selection to senior year financial aid applications. The strategies outlined here should inform decisions at every step, whether you're evaluating AP courses, researching dual credit opportunities, or maximizing FAFSA benefits. Remember that each choice, from early academic planning to financial aid optimization, contributes to your ultimate goal of affordable higher education.

The chapters have been designed to help you create and maintain a personalized college funding strategy. Use them annually to track progress and adjust your approach as circumstances change. Remember the Thompson family's FAFSA success story and Rachel's thoughtful college selection process; these examples demonstrate how understanding and utilizing available tools can lead to significant savings without compromising educational goals.

As you continue your college planning journey, strategy is key. Consider how different funding sources can work together; perhaps combining AP credits with local scholarships, or matching work-study opportunities with strategic course selection. The Chen family's remarkable achievement in reducing their college costs by over $100,000 shows how multiple strategies, when carefully coordinated, can yield impressive results.

Your path to affordable higher education is unique, but the tools and strategies shared in this book provide a framework for making informed decisions at every stage. Whether you're starting early with a 529 plan or seeking last-minute scholarship opportunities, remember that each step toward planning and preparing for college costs contributes to your larger goal. With careful planning, persistent effort, and strategic use of the resources available to you, achieving an affordable college education is within reach.

Bibliography

[1] Hurley J. (2023, August 16). *Coverdell Education Savings Account (ESA) vs. 529 Plan: Which Is Right for You?*. Saving For College. https://www.savingforcollege.com/article/coverdell-esa-versus-529-plan

[2] Kawashima, C. (2025, April 10). *Comparing Education Savings Accounts*. Charles Schwab. https://www.schwab.com/learn/story/comparing-education-savings-accounts

[3] KeyBank. (2025, March). *529 College Savings Plan vs. Coverdell Education Savings: What's the Difference?*. KeyBank. https://www.key.com/personal/banking101/529-vs-coverdell-esa.html

[4] Sadej, E. (2023). *The Differences Between 529s and Coverdell ESAs*. Blueleaf. https://www.blueleaf.com/articles/the-differences-between-529s-and-coverdell-esas/

[5] Bissonnette Z. (2010, August 30). *Debt-Free U: How I Paid for an Outstanding College Education Without Loans, Scholarships, or Mooching Off My Parents*. Goodreads. https://www.goodreads.com/book/show/7877387

[6] MacDonald, S. (2020). *Education Without Debt*. Author Scott MacDonald. https://authorscottmacdonald.com/education-without-debt-book/

[7] Lucyk S. (2025, March 28). *Dual Enrollment vs. AP Classes: Here's How to Decide*. Appily. https://www.appily.com/guidance/articles/applying-to-college/dual-enrollment-vs-ap-classes

[8] Western Kentucky University. (2017). *Advanced Placement or Dual Credit: Which Course Should You Take?*. Western Kentucky University. https://www.wku.edu/gifted/ap/ap-or-dual-credit.pdf

[9] College Board. (2024). *What's the difference between AP and dual enrollment programs?*. AP Students. https://apstudents.collegeboard.org/help-center/difference-ap-dual-enrollment

[10] Word In Black. (2023, May 01). *Is Dual Enrollment or AP Better for Earning College Credit?*. The Atlanta Voice. https://theatlantavoice.com/is-dual-enrollment-or-ap-better-for-earning-college-credit/

[11] Lydian Academy. (2021, December). *Educational Benefits of Early College Programs in High School*. Lydian Academy. https://lydianacademy.com/educational-benefits-of-early-college-programs-in-high-school/

[12] American Institutes for Research. (2020, February). *The Lasting Benefits of Early College High Schools Considerations and Recommendations for Policymakers*. American Institutes for Research. https://www.air.org/sites/default/files/downloads/report/Lasting-Benefits-Early-College-High-Schools-Brief-Feb-2020.pdf

[13] Bell, L. (2019, January 8). *The impact of early colleges: What does the research say?*. EducationNC. https://www.ednc.org/the-difference-early-college-makes/

[14] Fort Bend Independent School District. (2024, February 11). *Early College High School*. Fort Bend ISD. https://www.fortbendisd.com/domain/15898

[15] Atchison D., Zeiser K. L., Mohammed S., Levin J., Knight D. (2019, December). *The Costs and Benefits of Early College High Schools*. American Institutes for Research. https://www.echs-nm.com/wp-content/uploads/2020/04/Costs-Benefits-Early-College-High-Schools-508-report-Dec-2019.pdf

[16] College Scholarships. (2023, December 15). *Reviewed - Financial Aid Books*. CollegeScholarships.com. https://www.collegescholarships.com/pages/financialaidbooks

[17] Stevens, R. (2020, June 18). *Say No! To College Debt: Discover how you can graduate free of loans and eliminate the debt you have accumulated*. Barnes & Noble. https://www.barnesandnoble.com/w/say-no-to-college-debt-russ-stevens/1137200792

[18] Federal Student Aid. (2024, January 18). *What information will I need to fill out a FAFSA® form?*. Federal Student Aid. https://studentaid.gov/help/info-needed

[19] Federal Student Aid. (2023, December 31). *Filling Out the FAFSA Form*. Federal Student Aid. https://studentaid.gov/apply-for-aid/fafsa/filling-out

[20] Knight Randolph K. (2024, November 19). *2025-26 FAFSA Checklist: What You'll Need to Complete Your Application*. Fastweb. https://www.fastweb.com/financial-aid/articles/fafsa-checklist

[21] U.S. Department of Education. (2024, January 01). *2025-26 Free Application for Federal Student Aid (FAFSA)*. Federal Student Aid. https://studentaid.gov/sites/default/files/2025-26-fafsa.pdf

[22] Federal Student Aid. (2022, December 07). *Expected Family Contribution (EFC)*. FSA Partners Knowledge Center. https://fsapartners.ed.gov/knowledge-center/fsa-handbook/2023-2024/application-and-verification-guide/ch3-expected-family-contribution-efc

[23] FinAid. (2023, December 31). *Expected Family Contribution (EFC) Calculator*. FinAid.org. https://finaid.org/calculators/finaidestimate/

[24] Kantrowitz M. (2024, March 20). *What is the Expected Family Contribution (EFC)?*. Saving For College. https://www.savingforcollege.com/article/what-is-the-expected-family-contribution-efc

[25] Ascent. (2025, February 25). *EFC Meaning: What Happened to EFC?*. Ascent Blog. https://www.ascentfunding.com/blog/expected-family-contribution-efc-for-the-upcoming-school-year/

[26] Federal Student Aid. (2023, December 31). *What should I do if I have special financial circumstances?*. Federal Student Aid. https://studentaid.gov/help/reporting-special-financial-circumstances

[27] University of Cincinnati Student Financial Aid Office. (2024, January 01). *Special Circumstances*. University of Cincinnati. https://www.uc.edu/about/financial-aid/tools-resources/appeals/special-circumstances.html

[28] Federal Student Aid. (2023, March 16). *Special Cases*. Federal Student Aid Partner Connect. https://fsapartners.ed.gov/knowledge-center/fsa-handbook/2023-2024/application-and-verification-guide/ch5-special-cases

[29] Office of Student Financial Aid. (2022). *Special Circumstances Appeal Process*. University of Maryland Office of Student Financial Aid. https://financialaid.umd.edu/resources-policies/special-circumstances-appeal-process

[30] University of North Dakota. (2024). *Special Circumstances for Appealing FAFSA Eligibility*. University of North Dakota. https://und.edu/one-stop/financial-aid/special-circumstances.html

[31] Brookdale Community College. (2023). *Transferring with an Associate of Arts or Associate of Science Degree*. Brookdale Community College. https://www.brookdalecc.edu/documents/transfer-services/transfernjbrochure.pdf

[32] NJ Transfer Initiative. (2025). *Frequently Asked Questions*. NJTransfer.org. https://www.njtransfer.org/faq/

[33] Community College of Philadelphia. (2024, April). *Transfer Opportunities*. Community College of Philadelphia.

https://www.ccp.edu/student-services/academic-support-services/transfer-opportunities

34 Community College Research Center. (2021, July). *Community College Transfer*. Community College Research Center, Teachers College, Columbia University. https://ccrc.tc.columbia.edu/publications/community-college-transfer.html

35 U.S. Department of Veterans Affairs. (2025, February 26). *Post-9/11 GI Bill (Chapter 33)*. VA.gov. https://www.va.gov/education/about-gi-bill-benefits/post-9-11/

36 Military.com. (2024, January 01). *GI Bill*. Military.com. https://www.military.com/education/gi-bill

37 U.S. Army. (2023). *GI Bill*. GoArmy.com. https://www.goarmy.com/benefits/while-you-serve/education-training/gi-bill

38 (n.d.) https://ticas.org/wp-content/uploads/2021/07/Student-debt-metrics.pdf

39 The Institute for College Access & Success. (2023, April). *Paving the Path to Debt-Free College*. The Institute for College Access & Success. https://ticas.org/wp-content/uploads/2023/04/Paving-the-Path-to-Debt-Free-College.pdf

40 Howarth R. and Stifler L. (2019, March). *The Failings of Online For-profit Colleges: Findings from Student Borrower Focus Groups*. Brookings Institution. https://www.brookings.edu/wp-

content/uploads/2019/03/The-Failings-of-Online-For-profit-Colleges.pdf

[41] Garrett R. (2019). *Future Formula: Can Online Learning Help Solve College Debt?* Encoura. https://encoura.org/resources/wake-up-call/future-formula-the-quest-for-cheap-quality-productive-higher-education

[42] Review of Optometry. (2022, September). *NECO Initiatives Tackle Student Debt, Access to Education.* Review of Optometry. https://www.reviewofoptometry.com/article/neco-initiatives-tackle-student-debt-access-to-education

[43] Kumok Z. (2025, May 2). *Scholarships for High School Juniors.* Scholarships.com. https://www.scholarships.com/financial-aid/college-scholarships/scholarships-by-grade-level/high-school-scholarships/scholarships-for-high-school-juniors

[44] Bold.org. (2024, January 15). *Access Exclusive Local Scholarships.* Bold.org. https://bold.org/scholarships/by-state/

[45] Communities Foundation of Texas. (2025, January 15). *Apply for scholarships toward your academic goal.* Communities Foundation of Texas. https://cftexas.org/scholarships/apply-for-scholarships/

[46] SmarterSelect. (2020, April). *The Best 9 Scholarship Management Software (With Reviews Of Each).* SmarterSelect. https://info.smarterselect.com/the-best-9-scholarship-management-software

[47] Capterra. (2024, January 15). *Scholarship Management Software*. Capterra. https://www.capterra.com/scholarship-management-software/

[48] Scholarship Services Inc. (2025). *Win more scholarships with less effort*. ScholarshipOwl. https://scholarshipowl.com

[49] Spear E. (2020, January). *29 Key Performance Indicators (KPIs) for Colleges & Universities*. Precision Campus. https://precisioncampus.com/blog/education-kpis/

[50] Collegis Education. (2024, April). *Higher Education Program Evaluation: A Strategic Guide*. Collegis Education. https://collegiseducation.com/insights/higher-education-program-evaluation-a-strategic-guide/

[51] Hanover Research. (2023, April). *Best Practices: Program Evaluation and KPIs*. Inside Higher Ed. https://www.insidehighered.com/sites/default/files/2023-05/Best%20Practices%20-%20Program%20Evaluation%20and%20KPIs%20(1).pdf

[52] Usher, A. (2021, November 30). *Measuring Quality as if Quality Mattered*. Higher Education Strategy Associates. https://higheredstrategy.com/measuring-quality-as-if-quality-mattered/

[53] Aspen Institute College Excellence Program. (2023). *Measures of Student Success | Full Metrics*. Aspen Institute. https://highered.aspeninstitute.org/media/883

54 EducationData.org. (2024, January 01). *Average Cost of College*. EducationData.org. https://educationdata.org/average-cost-of-college

55 National Center for Education Statistics. (2024). *Tuition costs of colleges and universities.* Fast Facts. https://nces.ed.gov/fastfacts/display.asp?id=76

56 Tufts University Financial Services. (2024). *Undergraduate Cost of Attendance.* Tufts University Student Services. https://students.tufts.edu/financial-services/undergrad-aid/award-letter/undergraduate-cost-attendance

57 Welding L. (2024, December 20). *Average Cost of College: Facts and Statistics.* BestColleges.com. https://www.bestcolleges.com/research/average-cost-of-college/

58 Linton D. E. (2023, August 08). *Crushed: How Student Debt Has Impaired a Generation and What to Do About It.* Barnes & Noble. https://www.barnesandnoble.com/w/crushed-david-e-linton/1142553486

59 Curley P. (2019, October 01). *Executive Summary Question and Answer with Anthony ONeal, Author of Debt Free Degree by Ramsey Press.* 529 Conference. https://www.529conference.com/executive-summary-question-and-answer-with-anthony-oneal-author-of-debt-free-degree-by-ramsey-press/

60 U.S. Department of Veterans Affairs. (2025, March 3). *Post-9/11 GI Bill (Chapter 33) rates.* VA.gov. https://www.va.gov/education/benefit-rates/post-9-11-gi-bill-rates/

[61] U.S. Department of Veterans Affairs. (2025, February 12). *Future rates for Post-9/11 GI Bill*. VA.gov. https://www.va.gov/education/benefit-rates/post-9-11-gi-bill-rates/future-rates/

[62] Shane III, L. (2025, March 06). *What troops need to know about the GI Bill, tuition assistance in 2025*. Military Times. https://www.militarytimes.com/news/your-military/2025/03/06/what-troops-need-to-know-about-the-gi-bill-tuition-assistance-in-2025/

[63] Hersey L. F. (2025, January 03). *VA expands education benefits by a year for qualifying veterans with multiple enlistments*. Stars and Stripes. https://www.stripes.com/veterans/2025-01-03/veterans-education-benefits-gi-bills-16363592.html

[64] National Collegiate Athletic Association. (2014, October 24). *Play Division I Sports*. NCAA.org. https://www.ncaa.org/sports/2014/10/24/play-division-i-sports.aspx

[65] NCSA College Recruiting. (2024, January 15). *Athletic Scholarships: Everything You Need to Know*. NCSA Sports. https://www.ncsasports.org/recruiting/how-to-get-recruited/scholarship-facts

[66] Delesline III, N. (2023, April 12). *What Is An Athletic Scholarship?*. AffordableCollegesOnline.org. https://www.affordablecollegesonline.org/college-resource-center/how-do-athletic-scholarships-work/

[67] National Collegiate Athletic Association. (2024, August). *Guide for the College-Bound Student-Athlete*. NCAA Eligibility Center. http://fs.ncaa.org/Docs/eligibilitycenter/StudentResources/CBSA.pdf

[68] Honest Game. (2025, March 11). *Academic Eligibility 101 – Understanding the Academic Requirements for College Sports*. Honest Game. https://honestgame.com/blog/academic-eligibility-101/

[69] Federal Student Aid. (2023). *Federal Versus Private Student Loans*. StudentAid.gov. https://studentaid.gov/understand-aid/types/loans/federal-vs-private

[70] Martin A. (2024, December 05). *Federal vs. private student loans: What's the difference?*. Bankrate. https://www.bankrate.com/loans/student-loans/federal-vs-private-student-loans/

[71] Penn State University. (2025, January 01). *Comparing Federal and Private Student Loans*. Penn State University. https://www.psu.edu/costs-aid/types-of-aid/loans/comparing-federal-and-private-student-loans

[72] Investopedia. (2024, January 18). *Private vs. Federal College Loans: What's the Difference?*. Investopedia. https://www.investopedia.com/articles/younginvestors/09/private-or-federal-student-loans.asp

73 SmartAsset. (2025, March 13). *Pros and Cons of PLUS Loans for Parents*. SmartAsset. https://smartasset.com/student-loans/pros-and-cons-of-plus-loans-for-parents

74 Going Merry. (2024, June 11). *The Pros and Cons of Parent PLUS Loans*. Going Merry. https://goingmerry.com/blog/pros-and-cons-of-parent-plus-loans/

75 Iowa Student Loan. (2024, January 1). *Parent PLUS Loan Features, Benefits, and Drawbacks: What You Need to Know*. Iowa Student Loan Education Lending. https://www.iowastudentloan.org/articles/parents/parent-plus-loan-features.aspx

76 Bhakyapaibul, P. (2025, February 26). *Parent PLUS Loans: Eligibility, interest rates, and more*. Sallie Mae. https://www.salliemae.com/blog/what-is-a-parent-plus-loan/

77 Investopedia. (2023, December 15). *The Dangers of Taking Out a Direct PLUS Loan*. Investopedia. https://www.investopedia.com/articles/personal-finance/121015/dangers-taking-out-parent-plus-loan.asp

78 Federal Student Aid. (2023, December 31). *Federal Work-Study jobs help students earn money to pay for college or career school*. Federal Student Aid. https://studentaid.gov/understand-aid/types/work-study

79 Boucher, A. (2025, January 8). *Understanding federal work-study eligibility and the application process*. Sallie Mae.

https://www.sallie.com/resources/financial-aid/federal-work-study-eligibility-applications

[80] Student Financial Services. (2023, July 1). *Federal Work-Study Rules and Guidelines*. Columbia University Student Financial Services. https://sfs.columbia.edu/content/federal-work-study-rules-and-guidelines

[81] U.S. Department of Education. (2022, July 14). *The Federal Work-Study Program*. Federal Student Aid Partner Connect Knowledge Center. https://fsapartners.ed.gov/knowledge-center/fsa-handbook/2022-2023/vol6/ch2-federal-work-study-program

[82] Boston Architectural College. (2023). *Federal Work-Study (FWS) Program*. The Boston Architectural College. https://the-bac.edu/financial-aid/federal-work-study

[83] City College of San Francisco. (2024, January 1). *Office of (On-Campus) Student Employment*. City College of San Francisco. https://www.ccsf.edu/paying-college/office-campus-student-employment

[84] University of California. (2023, October 15). *Jobs & work-study*. University of California Admissions. https://admission.universityofcalifornia.edu/tuition-financial-aid/types-of-aid/jobs-and-work-study.html

[85] Angelo State University. (2024). *Your Guide to College Campus Jobs: Work, Study, and Beyond*. Angelo State University Blog. https://www.angelo.edu/live/blogs/work-study-and-on-campus-jobs

[86] Crossland, S. (2020, January 3). *Book Review: Debt-Free Degree: The Step-by-Step Guide to Getting Your Kid Through College Without Student Loans*. NASFAA. https://www.nasfaa.org/news-item/20488/BookReviewDebt-FreeDegreeTheStep-by-StepGuidetoGettingYourKidThroughCollegeWithoutStudent_Loans

[87] Bissonnette, Z. (2011). *Book Recommendation: Debt-Free U by Zac Bissonnette*. Being Good at Being Poor. https://beinggoodatbeingpoor.wordpress.com/book-recommendation-debt-free-u-by-zac-bissonnette/

[88] Kantrowitz, M. (2025, February 3). *How To Appeal for More Financial Aid for College*. Saving For College. https://www.savingforcollege.com/article/how-to-appeal-for-more-financial-aid-for-college

[89] Davidson, C. (2024, March 14). *Need More Financial Aid? Learn About the Appeal Process*. MEFA. https://www.mefa.org/article/need-financial-aid-learn-appeal-process/

[90] FinAid. (2023, October 15). *How to Appeal Financial Aid Award Packages*. FinAid.org. https://finaid.org/financial-aid-applications/financial-aid-appeal/

[91] Going Merry. (2025, January 29). *A Guide to Writing the Perfect Financial Aid Appeal Letter*. Going Merry. https://goingmerry.com/blog/financial-aid-appeal-letter/

92 Internal Revenue Service. (2025, January 13). *Education credits: Questions and answers*. IRS.gov. https://www.irs.gov/credits-deductions/individuals/education-credits-questions-and-answers

93 American Council on Education. (2025, April 22). *Tax Reform and Higher Education in 2025*. American Council on Education. https://www.acenet.edu/Policy-Advocacy/Pages/Tax-Reform-and-Higher-Education-2025.aspx

94 TurboTax Expert. (2025, March 03). *The Lowdown on Education Tax Breaks*. TurboTax. https://turbotax.intuit.com/tax-tips/college-and-education/the-lowdown-on-education-tax-breaks-/L5n9piNb4

95 UCI Financial Services. (2023, January 1). *About Education Tax Credits*. UCI Financial Services. https://fs.uci.edu/tax-information/about-tax-credits.php

96 Mowreader, A. (2024, August 26). *Cost of Course Materials Impacts Student Success*. Inside Higher Ed. https://www.insidehighered.com/news/student-success/health-wellness/2024/08/26/college-students-avoid-courses-high-textbook-costs

97 Esposito J. (2017, March 27). *How to Reduce the Cost of College Textbooks*. The Scholarly Kitchen. https://scholarlykitchen.sspnet.org/2017/03/27/reduce-cost-college-textbooks/

98 Arizona Central Credit Union. (2024, August 7). *6 Smart Strategies to Save on College Textbooks*. Arizona Central Credit Union.

https://www.azcentralcu.org/blog/smart-strategies-to-save-on-college-textbooks/

[99] Curtis J. (2025, January 28). *A Parent's Take on College Textbook Costs*. Pressbooks. https://pressbooks.com/news/a-parents-take-on-college-textbook-costs/

Thank You for Reading!

I hope you found *Don't Go Broke Paying for College* helpful and enjoyable!

Your feedback is invaluable to me and helps others discover this book.

If you could take a moment to **leave a review**, I'd greatly appreciate it. Scan the QR code below to leave your review:

Thank you,

Patty R. Adams

www.ingramcontent.com/pod-product-compliance
Lightning Source LLC
Chambersburg PA
CBHW061759120626
46550CB00005B/2061